JACQUI HONESS-MARTIN

Jacqui is a playwright and theatre director.

As Artistic Director of InSite Performance she has written and directed *We Have Fallen* (IdeasTap Underbelly Award, Edinburgh); *SMITH* (The British Museum); *Antigone* (Walworth Council Chambers); and directed *Abyss* and *Larisa and the Merchants* (Arcola Theatre).

Tell Out My Soul, her first original play, was staged at the Public Theatre New York in 2008.

She is currently Literary Associate at West Yorkshire Playhouse.

Other Titles in this Series

Mike Bartlett
BULL
GAME
AN INTERVENTION
KING CHARLES III

Tom Basden
THE CROCODILE
HOLES
JOSEPH K
THERE IS A WAR

Deborah Bruce
THE DISTANCE
GODCHILD
SAME

Jez Butterworth
JERUSALEM
JEZ BUTTERWORTH PLAYS: ONE
MOJO
THE NIGHT HERON
PARLOUR SONG
THE RIVER
THE WINTERLING

Caryl Churchill
BLUE HEART
CHURCHILL PLAYS: THREE
CHURCHILL PLAYS: FOUR
CHURCHILL: SHORTS
CLOUD NINE
DING DONG THE WICKED
A DREAM PLAY *after* Strindberg
DRUNK ENOUGH TO SAY
    I LOVE YOU?
FAR AWAY
HERE WE GO
HOTEL
ICECREAM
LIGHT SHINING IN
    BUCKINGHAMSHIRE
LOVE AND INFORMATION
MAD FOREST
A NUMBER
SEVEN JEWISH CHILDREN
THE SKRIKER
THIS IS A CHAIR
THYESTES *after* Seneca
TRAPS

Paul Davies
FIREBIRD

Vivienne Franzmann
MOGADISHU
PESTS
THE WITNESS

James Fritz
ROSS & RACHEL

debbie tucker green
BORN BAD
DIRTY BUTTERFLY
HANG
NUT
RANDOM
STONING MARY
TRADE & GENERATIONS
TRUTH AND RECONCILIATION

Rose Heiney
ELEPHANTS

Ella Hickson
THE AUTHORISED KATE BANE
BOYS
EIGHT
GIFT
PRECIOUS LITTLE TALENT
    & HOT MESS
WENDY & PETER PAN *after* Barrie

Vicky Jones
THE ONE

Anna Jordan
CHICKEN SHOP
FREAK
YEN

Lucy Kirkwood
BEAUTY AND THE BEAST
    with Katie Mitchell
BLOODY WIMMIN
CHIMERICA
HEDDA *after* Ibsen
IT FELT EMPTY WHEN THE
    HEART WENT AT FIRST BUT
    IT IS ALRIGHT NOW
NSFW
TINDERBOX

Cordelia Lynn
LELA & CO.

Evan Placey
CONSENSUAL
GIRLS LIKE THAT
GIRLS LIKE THAT & OTHER PLAYS
    FOR TEENAGERS
PRONOUN

Kat Roberts
STAYING ALIVE

Ali Taylor
COTTON WOOL
FAULT LINES
THE MACHINE GUNNERS
    after Robert Westall
OVERSPILL

Jack Thorne
2ND MAY 1997
BUNNY
BURYING YOUR BROTHER IN
    THE PAVEMENT
HOPE
JACK THORNE PLAYS: ONE
LET THE RIGHT ONE IN
    after John Ajvide Lindqvist
MYDIDAE
THE SOLID LIFE OF SUGAR WATER
STACY & FANNY AND FAGGOT
WHEN YOU CURE ME

Phoebe Waller-Bridge
FLEABAG

Tom Wells
JUMPERS FOR GOALPOSTS
THE KITCHEN SINK
ME, AS A PENGUIN

Jacqui Honess-Martin

PINE

NICK HERN BOOKS

London

www.nickhernbooks.co.uk

A Nick Hern Book

Pine first published in Great Britain in 2015 as a paperback original by Nick Hern Books Limited, The Glasshouse, 49a Goldhawk Road, London W12 8QP

Pine copyright © 2015 Jacqui Honess-Martin

Jacqui Honess-Martin has asserted her moral right to be identified as the author of this work

Cover image: © iStock.com/greg801

Designed and typeset by Nick Hern Books, London
Printed in Great Britain by Mimeo Ltd, Huntingdon, Cambridgeshire PE29 6XX

A CIP catalogue record for this book is available from the British Library

ISBN   978 1 84842 548 4

Woodland CARBON
www.woodlandcarbon.co.uk
NICK HERN BOOKS
Printed on Carbon Captured paper

Pine was first performed at Hampstead Theatre Downstairs, London, on 10 December 2015. The cast was as follows:

GABBY	Hannah Britland
JOE	Matt Whitchurch
BETTY	Lucy May Barker
TAJ	Ronak Patani
SAMI	David Mumeni

Director	Lisa Spirling
Designer	Polly Sullivan
Lighting	Johanna Town
Sound and Music	Barnaby Race
Assistant Director	Leah Fogo
Stage Manager	Annette Waldie

Acknowledgements

With thanks to Will Mortimer, all at Hampstead Theatre, Ben Addis, and Lisa Spirling.

J.H-M.

For Ben

8

Characters

GABBY, *twenty-five, female, the manager of Festive Pines*
JOE, *twenty-three, male, rugby player, Welsh, the assistant
    manager*
BETTY, *twenty-one, female, London local*
TAJ, *twenty-two, male, London local*
SAMI, *thirty-ish, male, Taj's cousin, the area manager*

The Setting

December this year, a car park in an affluent London 'village',
transformed annually into a large Christmas-tree store, Festive
Pines.

Notes on Staging

The audience never see the customers. They are, however, seen
and interacted with clearly by the staff. Dialogue directed to
customers is denoted by bold text.

Notes on Text

/ denotes an interruption and overlap of subsequent dialogue

– against a character is a lack of response where one is expected

… is an uncompleted thought

Note on Songs

This text went to press before song choices had been finalised. The original production used contemporary Christmas pop songs, standards, and traditional carols in arrangements by Barnaby Race. Though songs are suggested for certain characters, these can be supported or sung by the whole company.

This text went to press before the end of rehearsals and so may differ slightly from the play as performed.

ACT ONE

'Song One' – Gabby

Scene One

Sunday 29th November.

GABBY *is holding a tree upright as* SAMI *measures it.* TAJ *is in the corner, unnoticed.*

SAMI. So what height would you say this is then?

GABBY. Five foot.

SAMI. Babe, see, this is the issue we had last year.

GABBY. I wonder if I shouldn't be in charge?

SAMI. Graduate like you, I think you'll be okay. What did you study again?

GABBY. You know what I /

SAMI. Writing, wasn't it?

GABBY. English literature and language.

SAMI. When you / speak the English language.

GABBY. Speak the English language. Yes.

SAMI. It's your mother tongue.

GABBY. Yes.

SAMI. Thirty grand to study a language you already speak.

GABBY. It really tickles you, doesn't it?

SAMI. Cracks me up.

GABBY. Still. After all these years.

SAMI. You measure to the crown, yeah? Then, half of the leader and then you round up if it's past six inches and down if it's less. Cos six inches is half. So what's this?

GABBY. Six foot.

SAMI. You are going to win 'Best Outlet' this year, I have faith in you, Gabs – I believe!

GABBY. Do you want me to slice your eyes out with this Stanley knife now or make it part of training?

SAMI. Won't slice nothing with that one, babes, blade's blunt, they all are. Health and safety innit.

GABBY. I thought you were in Clapham today.

SAMI. The only female boss in a male-dominated industry, you could write an article about that maybe.

GABBY. Yes.

SAMI. About how you are breaking balls and that.

GABBY. Yes.

SAMI. So you can stop eating the chocolates in the lucky dip, now you're in charge, yeah? They're for the kids. Set an example.

GABBY. Actually, Sam, could I change my mind about that?

SAMI. Everyone has to have a lucky dip. It's tradition.

GABBY. About being the manager.

SAMI. You don't want to do it?

GABBY. I think what I'd like is to just keep things casual, not stocktake and do rota problems and cash up and have to do Christmas Eve /

SAMI. You'll be fine. It's your last time, isn't it?

GABBY. Yes.

SAMI. Really this time, not like last year and the year before and the /

GABBY. Yes.

SAMI. Unless you want to set us up an empire out there?

GABBY. No, thank you.

SAMI. We're expanding, you know?

GABBY. To Germany?

SAMI. Surrey.

GABBY. –

SAMI. I've got a full-time job for someone. Keep your eyes open, let me know who's good. I've got high hopes for this Joe guy, make him your assistant manager.

GABBY. Why not make Taj the manager?

SAMI. Because his Asperger's scares the children.

GABBY. Sami.

SAMI. Just keep him out back.

GABBY. You can't keep saying he's autistic, he isn't.

SAMI. It's the spectrum though innit.

GABBY. What? No. He's /

SAMI. Nothing like as smart as he thinks he is, that's the trouble.

GABBY. Not like you.

SAMI. School of life.

GABBY. Don't say that.

SAMI. What?

GABBY. School of / life.

SAMI. What?

GABBY. You sound like such a bitter / old man.

SAMI. I'm bitter? You looked in the mirror at your face lately?

GABBY. All right. Who else is there?

SAMI. This Joe guy and some student called Elizabeth – oh! You're gonna love this: the most important new member of the team, da-dah!

GABBY. Who?

SAMI. Here! Speakers!

GABBY. What for?

SAMI. Outdoor ones. So you don't have to listen to that crappy little radio.

GABBY. We can play the radio on these?

SAMI. Nah, for Christmas stuff.

GABBY. No way. Come on, Sam, you're not here every day.

SAMI. The customers like it.

GABBY. They hate it, they get it everywhere.

SAMI. It improves sales.

GABBY. What about staff morale?

SAMI. What's more cheering than Slade?

GABBY. A bath of boiling oil.

SAMI. Don't make me regret promoting you.

GABBY. That is exactly what I'm trying / to do.

SAMI. Especially after last year /

GABBY. That was a misunderstanding.

SAMI. I had to work hard to smooth that over for you.

GABBY. No you didn't, I spoke to Big Nick, it was fine. The kid was asking for it.

SAMI. It's not your job to discipline other people's children.

GABBY. No, he got in the netter and he asked to be pushed through.

SAMI. He was four years old.

GABBY. We always put Taj through the netter. That's a tradition.

SAMI. Yeah, well, there is someone who is asking for it.

TAJ. I don't like it actually.

SAMI. How long have you been sitting there?

TAJ. About an hour.

SAMI. We start at ten.

TAJ. The bus only goes once an hour on a Sunday.

SAMI. You can walk it in fifteen, Jesus, what, too excited to stay in bed?

TAJ. I brought Gabby a coffee, I thought we could catch up.

SAMI. By sitting here staring at her?

TAJ. I wasn't expecting you to be here.

SAMI. Not over it yet then?

GABBY. Sami. Don't.

SAMI. Okay. I'll ask this Joe guy to manage.

GABBY. Thank you.

SAMI. You can earn five twenty-four an hour less, that's about forty-two pounds a day, which is just over a grand all-in.

GABBY. It's an extra thousand pounds?

SAMI. Thirteen hundred euro. You can be bossed around all day by some bloke who's never done it before, that make you feel happier?

GABBY. It's not the money, it is the money / obviously, but I just – I just.

SAMI. When you called and begged me for this job again.

GABBY. I did not / beg, you just begged me.

SAMI. When you called and begged me for this job again I thought this year, unlike last year, we might be able to capture some of that original Christmas spirit, the wide-eyed joy and dedicated customer service you demonstrated when we first hired you.

GABBY. I'll look like I'm enjoying it if it makes you feel better.

TAJ. I bet you say that to all the girls. No, hear that from.

–

Fuck.

SAMI. You all right there, autism? I can feel my Christmas
    Tingle coming on.

GABBY. That's sexual harassment.

SAMI. If you have other offers of employment.

GABBY. I don't. You know I don't.

SAMI. No? I can't think why.

GABBY. This was supposed to be a one-off, temporary thing.
    Three years later, I'm the manager.

SAMI. That's how I started out.

GABBY. Yes. I – know. I remember. I keep expecting Ed to be
    at the netter.

SAMI. Hear that, Taj? She misses her boyfriend. How's he
    doing out there?

GABBY. Good. He finished his internship, he's setting up this
    graphic-design thing with a friend.

SAMI. Give him my best, won't you? Tell him he's sorely
    missed.

GABBY. I will.

SAMI. What are you going to do out there?

GABBY. I don't know.

SAMI. Do you speak German?

GABBY. Yes. No. A bit. It's very hard.

SAMI. Harder than the English language?

GABBY. Yes, objectively people say it's harder than learning
    English.

SAMI. So you studied English, which you already speak, to be a
    journalist in England. And now you're going to do 'you don't
    know what' in Germany when you don't speak any German?

GABBY. I can't get a job as a journalist here, can I?

SAMI. Well, that's a silver lining cos it means you get to be here
    doing this job with me, so stop looking like you've swallowed
    Jimmy Savile and let's get a little festive spirit going, yeah?

GABBY. You're the worst Muslim I ever met.

SAMI. What, out of him and me? Good.

GABBY. I know more Muslims that just you two.

TAJ. No you don't.

SAMI. I don't care. Cheer the fuck up.

TAJ. Only six weeks to go, Gabs.

GABBY. Thanks, Taj.

BETTY *enters*.

BETTY. Hello.

GABBY. Hi.

SAMI. You must be Elizabeth, welcome.

BETTY. I prefer Betty.

SAMI. That's pretty.

BETTY. It's classic.

SAMI. That's Gabby, she's been here years.

GABBY. This is my fourth / year.

SAMI. That's Taj.

TAJ. Season's greetings.

BETTY. Wow, it's huge, there's so many trees.

SAMI. We have the best range in the area. You're studying, right?

BETTY. Why else would you do this?

SAMI. Yeah, Taj is studying too.

BETTY. Where are you?

TAJ. Leeds.

BETTY. Shut up!

TAJ. Sorry.

BETTY. That's where I am! I've not seen you around. Do you
    go to Mission or Tiger Tiger?

TAJ. Why are you saying it twice?

SAMI. Taj is a post-grad genius.

BETTY. Oh, you're post-grad, okay.

TAJ. I'm waiting to hear on the funding for my PhD.

  JOE *enters*.

SAMI. Joe my man.

JOE. Hi, Sami, is it?

SAMI. Welcome to Festive Pines.

JOE. I thought you were a girl from the emails.

SAMI. What?

JOE. Sami with an 'i' like Bobbi or – Anyway, you're not, hi.
  Nice to meet you, mate.

BETTY. Hi! I'm Betty. With a 'y'.

JOE. I thought it was a bit odd, cos the manager has to be here
  on their own.

SAMI. Yeah?

JOE. Yeah, I mean, what if a customer comes in and wants a
  fifteen-foot tree?

GABBY. Then he will have to help lift it into the car, same as
  he would anyone.

JOE. What if it's a woman?

GABBY. Trust me, only men buy the fifteen-foot ones.

SAMI. So this is Gabby, Gabs, Gabriel. Like the angel.

GABBY. I'm the manager. Hi.

JOE. Hello. Lovely to meet you.

GABBY. Charmed.

SAMI. The good news is: Joe, I'm promoting you!

JOE. Really?

GABBY. Really?

SAMI. Absolutely. That was insightful, strategic management stuff you had there. It's another two pounds thirteen an hour.

JOE. Thanks, Sam, that's great, you know I'm only here this year, right?

SAMI. Aren't you all? Not a problem.

TAJ. I'm Taj.

SAMI. I think this team's gonna manage something really special. Gabby's missed out on 'Best Outlet' three times now. So she's all out this year, right, Gabs?

GABBY. It's all I want for Christmas.

SAMI. Gabs is gonna take us through some training.

GABBY. Right. Okay. I thought you weren't staying.

SAMI. Nah, the bloke at Clapham's sound so.

GABBY. Thank you. Okay. We're going to be here about four hours and the training is how to use the till, how to measure and label the trees up correctly, the different types of tree we sell and how to net them. Which is really fun for the first, I dunno, ten trees.

BETTY. I just need to do the till training.

GABBY. Sorry?

BETTY. I can't lift the trees, so I'll be on the till.

GABBY. The till is inside, so everyone gets to have a go on the till.

BETTY. Yeah but, I can't lift a tree! Look at me.

GABBY. Are you hurt or – is something wrong / with.

BETTY. I agree with Joe.

GABBY. About what?

BETTY. I'm a girl.

GABBY. Yes.

BETTY. Right.

GABBY. Do you have any other shoes?

BETTY. I thought I was going to be on the till. Sitting. I mean, Joe can lift stuff, look at him.

GABBY. You'll need to dress warm but layers are best because it's physical work and you work up a sweat. If you can't lift the bigger trees you can ask for help, but it's mostly helping customers and everyone can do that.

BETTY. I just think my skills would be better utilised.

GABBY. You'll need layers and practical shoes.

BETTY. Like, what, yours?

GABBY. Walking boots or some people wear wellingtons.

BETTY. Oh great, I've got those. For Glastonbury.

GABBY. Great. So –

BETTY. It's just I think Joe might get bored of me asking for his help all the time.

GABBY. I cannot imagine a situation in which that would be in any way irritating for any of us. Something tells me Joe will cope, after all, it's Christmas.

JOE. I'll be fine.

GABBY. Good.

BETTY. Might as well put those lovely arms to some use.

GABBY (*sotto*). Christ.

JOE. Happy to help.

SAMI. That's the spirit.

GABBY. I'm afraid we don't see Sami very often, he only looks in on us every now and again, we don't see Big Nick, the owner, at all except for /

SAMI. Except for 'Best Outlet' Judging Day.

GABBY. Or as we like to call it: 'The Saviour's Day'.

SAMI. You remember that conversation we just had about your sarcasm?

GABBY. And this year as a special treat, there are speakers that play Slade.

BETTY. There's Christmas music?

TAJ. Can I still have Absolute Rock?

GABBY. Bon Jovi *or* Slade, happy day.

SAMI. Keep it classy, Christmas music with some classical or old-fashioned stuff. Not too much Wham! It's not Woolworths.

BETTY. What's Woolworths?

SAMI. –

GABBY. You greet every customer as they walk in the gate. If you say, 'Hi, do you know what you're looking for?' They will say, 'I'd like a tree please!' So, if you don't want to set that hilarious gag up for them after December 2nd, mind your syntax.

JOE. Fuck me.

GABBY. It means the construction of a sentence to create meaning.

JOE. Fifty-five pounds for a six-foot one.

GABBY. Oh that.

SAMI. Three-foot trees in blocks start at thirty-five, our twelve-foot firs, while they last, are a hundred and twenty pounds.

JOE. People spend a hundred and twenty pounds on a Christmas tree?

GABBY. It is the most wonderful time of the year.

JOE. Who's got room for a twelve-foot tree?

SAMI. The Fraser firs are the most expensive because they smell good and they look like the trees we had when we were kids.

JOE. We had a plastic one.

TAJ. What tree did Auntie Sal let in the house when you were a kid?

SAMI. People round here don't mind paying for quality.

BETTY. We always get our trees here.

JOE. It's pretty quiet though, right, until mid-December?

GABBY. From this week it's pubs, offices, businesses, the big trees, then our really crazy weekends are the first two in December, depending when the dates fall. We don't usually have much stock after December 15th.

JOE. We sell out?

GABBY. Sometimes.

JOE. Wow.

SAMI. This is where families come in their Audi Estates on that first December Saturday morning when the posh schools break up to spend time choosing something really special. Choosing it and being here, kids running round, the lucky dip, the mistletoe, the music, it's part of the experience. We provide the magical start to the festive season.

GABBY. And the opportunity to spend more than half the weekly national minimum wage on a dead shrub.

SAMI. Most people spend fifty quid. It's the opposite to bartering on the street corner with some Hungarian migrant. I'll do till training.

GABBY. Please.

BETTY. Oh great.

BETTY *and* SAMI *go into the cabin.*

JOE. Can we start again?

GABBY. Hello. Sorry I'm a girl.

JOE. I'm very happy you're a girl.

GABBY. I have a boyfriend called Ed. He's in Germany and I fly out there on January 4th.

JOE. I didn't mean it like that.

Beat.

I'm all for women's lib.

GABBY. Is it 1912?

JOE. Equality.

GABBY. Good.

JOE. Do they have security at night to look after you when you're locking up?

GABBY. How do you know I can't take care of myself?

JOE. Fair play. You could be a kung fu master.

GABBY. I could be, yes.

JOE. But you still can't lift a fifteen-foot tree on your own.

GABBY. What do you bench-press?

JOE. Ninety-five.

GABBY. That's exactly what I do.

JOE. Kilograms?

GABBY. Yeah.

JOE. I expect you lift ninety-five pounds which is okay. For a girl.

GABBY. I think it's kilograms.

JOE. I weigh ninety kilograms. Think you could lift me? I'll run up you can catch me.

GABBY. I don't need to kiss my guns every morning to be able to look after myself or provide good customer service. I've been doing this three years. I'm fine.

JOE. You've been doing this three years?

GABBY. Yes.

JOE. Wow. Sorry, I thought it was just like an in-between thing for most people.

GABBY. It is. It is an in-between thing for me.

JOE. Between what?

TAJ. If I just ran at you what would happen?

GABBY. Taj! Stop lurking.

TAJ. I know how to use the till.

GABBY. Journalist.

JOE. Who for?

GABBY. I'm freelance. Christmas is slow for... news. What about you?

JOE. I'm a scrum half.

BETTY *enters*.

BETTY. Your turn, Joe.

GABBY. What's that?

JOE. It's a position in rugby.

BETTY. I had you down as a winger. I'm a student.

JOE. I should go look at this till.

JOE *leaves*.

BETTY. He is: So. Hot.

TAJ. He wouldn't even wobble, would he?

BETTY. No. God I love rugby boys.

GABBY. He plays rugby for a living? Can you do that?

BETTY. I can tell what sport all boys play just by looking at them.

GABBY. He just told you what he plays.

TAJ. What about me?

BETTY. Badminton?

TAJ. That's very good.

BETTY. This month is going to be fun.

GABBY. Why is he here if he plays rugby for a living?

BETTY. He means he plays rugby at uni, some of those teams are really serious.

GABBY. Oh right, of course, why didn't he just say, 'I do sports science at Shitville Met' then?

BETTY. So are you like the manager all year round?

GABBY. Yeah, it's pretty quiet in July.

TAJ. She's being sarcastic, you learn to spot it. Big Nick's the owner and Sami started off working like us and now he manages growers and suppliers the rest of the year. But not like all year. I think he makes enough in December to take January to June off.

BETTY. Wow.

TAJ. While the rest of us sweat away in the library.

BETTY. Oh no, I'm doing sociology. My dad made me get a job because I graduate next year and he says I need some work experience. I applied for loads of stuff in the city but I didn't even get a response to my CV.

GABBY. That's shocking.

BETTY. I know. I mean, youth unemployment, blah, blah, but I was Head Girl.

GABBY. That's crazy.

BETTY. I know. Can I talk to you about some days off? I have to go ice-skating on Saturday 12th.

GABBY. No one gets Saturdays off.

BETTY. It's Somerset House.

GABBY. Sorry.

BETTY. Do people really buy trees from next weekend?

GABBY. Hundreds of them.

BETTY. I love Christmas trees. It's always the best part, isn't it? Choosing one and decorating it. I love that.

GABBY. I've not had one for the past couple of years.

BETTY. What's your favourite bit of Christmas, Tak?

TAJ. Taj.

BETTY. What?

TAJ. My name is Taj.

BETTY. Oh. Where's that from?

TAJ. My parents gave it to me.

SAMI *and* JOE *enter.*

BETTY. Where are you studying, Joe?

JOE. I didn't go to uni.

BETTY. Oh.

SAMI. Waste of money.

GABBY. Netters next or measuring?

BETTY. Wait. You're a professional rugby player?

JOE. I've just finished a contract with the Harlequins.

BETTY. Oh my God.

GABBY. Betty, we need to go and look at the netter now.

BETTY. Joe plays for the London Harlequins!

SAMI. That's pretty impressive.

JOE. I did.

GABBY. Did they teach you to use a netter?

BETTY. Gabby, you must have heard of the Harlequins.

GABBY. Italian clowns.

BETTY. No they're in London because they're called the London Harlequins.

GABBY. The netter is great for your core muscles.

BETTY. Unless it's like Surrey Cricket.

TAJ. You're good then?

BETTY. I'll google it.

JOE. I'm all right, yeah.

GABBY. So I'm told.

BETTY. Oh my God. My brother is going to go spare when I tell him. You must have been on the TV and everything.

JOE. No international call-up yet.

GABBY. And we still have measuring to go.

TAJ. Why are you here then? If you're a famous rugby player?

JOE. I'm not famous.

GABBY. So we'd best crack on.

BETTY. Oh my days! There you are, see!

GABBY. No phones allowed on site.

JOE. I'm injured at the minute.

BETTY. God, you poor thing. If you need a massage just say, I've got healing hands.

SAMI. You need to declare any pre-existing injury for our insurance, cos you're on zero hours so we don't / cover you.

JOE. No, it's fine. It doesn't affect anything else. Just rugby.

GABBY. Don't they pay you when you're injured?

JOE. It's a bit complicated and the money's nothing like football unless you're Leigh Halfpenny.

BETTY. Oh my God. I love Leigh Halfpenny.

GABBY. When do you get a new contract?

JOE. New year. Hopefully.

SAMI. Well, if that falls through and you want to make some serious cash after this, give me a shout, yeah?

JOE. What, selling trees after Christmas?

BETTY. I'm on nine pounds eight pence an hour. What serious cash?

SAMI. On the management side of things, suppliers and that.

GABBY. You're offering him the job?

SAMI. I'm keeping my eyes open for talent, Gabs. We're expanding next year, I'm going to need another pair of hands.

GABBY. You've only known him four minutes.

SAMI. I can spot talent.

JOE. Thanks, mate, but I'll be back on a pitch somewhere by then.

BETTY. Going back to play for England I reckon.

Beat.

GABBY. We call the rat Maz.

BETTY. What?

GABBY. We have rats.

TAJ. A rat.

GABBY. Yeah, it's definitely the same one. She's called Maz.

TAJ. So there's just one.

GABBY. We gave her a name so she's less frightening for Taj and so we can warn each other where she is without letting the customers know.

TAJ. We say, 'Watch out for Maz, she's in the six-foot Nordmann rack.' Especially if there are kids.

BETTY. Jesus.

TAJ. We thought about that, but it felt potentially offensive and it would probably draw more attention to say 'Jesus is in the potted three-footers,' than just screaming, 'Fuck there's a rat.'

SAMI. Should I put an extra page in the manual or is this not in the official training?

GABBY. No one seemed very interested in the netter.

JOE. So what exactly does good customer service mean at Festive Pines?

SAMI. Great question, Joe.

GABBY. You show people where things are and hold trees out for them. Shake the branches out and give it a spin.

JOE. Could you show us?

GABBY. What?

JOE. Show us, like, how you do the magical festive-spirit thing. As you've been here three years.

GABBY. How do you want me to / show you?

SAMI. The guy at Clapham does a role-play thing.

GABBY. Then go to fucking Clapham!

SAMI. Would you like to see a little role-play, Joe?

JOE. Love to.

GABBY. Okay. What, with Joe or – ?

SAMI. Just do it I reckon.

GABBY. I need someone to be the customer.

JOE. Well, no one knows what they're doing yet, we need you to show us.

GABBY. Sami.

SAMI. You can do it, doesn't need me.

GABBY. What, into thin air?

SAMI. Show us your powers of imagination.

Beat.

GABBY *acts out, as best she can, an encounter with an imaginary customer.*

GABBY. Hello. Welcome to Festive Pines, my name is Gabby, I'm the manager here, are you familiar with our range of Grade-A firs and spruces? Each has a different look and texture, they're all non-drop, some have a stronger fragrance… Do you know what size tree you're looking for? We price by height. We also have a range of festive decorations, like our holly wreaths and woven willow reindeer.

BETTY. Three years? Really?

GABBY. There's nobody there!

SAMI. All right, they get the idea; do it better than that. We have to stocktake and label up after deliveries and someone has to be on the till and cash up and keep things neat and tidy and that's it.

GABBY. And sometimes someone has to be a car-park attendant because it gets full.

BETTY. Can I not do that either?

JOE. The netter looks fun though.

TAJ. It isn't.

SAMI. Take turns on the till so no one gets too cold or wet, give the girls longer shifts indoors or they moan.

GABBY. It's physical and it's hard work.

SAMI. But she keeps coming back.

JOE. We doing the netter then?

GABBY. You put the trees in trunk first and pull. That's it.

SAMI. I'll do measuring, as I'm here.

Everyone files out. JOE *hangs back with* GABBY.

JOE. So what, brown-belt judo? Fight club?

GABBY. The security guard is called Stephen and his Alsatian is called Sheryl. Sometimes she shits behind the hay bales.

JOE. I feel better not locking up on my own.

GABBY. You okay doing another job whilst you're injured?

JOE. It'll keep me fit. I hate the gym too. It'll be fun.

GABBY. Yes, by December 23rd, Taj will convert and bless everyone, Betty will get her wings and we'll be hopelessly in love.

Pause.

JOE. It's definitely pounds by the way.

GABBY. Yes. Obviously.

JOE. Nice to meet you. Merry Christmas.

GABBY. Don't say that.

JOE. Merry / Christmas?

GABBY. It's November. There's only so much 'merry' to go round: you're starting too early.

JOE. I didn't realise I could wear it out.

GABBY. Welcome to Festive Pines.

JOE. Happy New Year then?

GABBY. I'll keep you posted.

TAJ (*off*). Gabby! GABBY!

JOE. Is that Maz?

GABBY. Oh God.

JOE. We okay then, yeah?

GABBY. Taj! Just stamp your feet or – it's a fucking pigeon, you moron.

'Song Two' – Joe

Scene Two

Saturday December 5th.

GABBY *and* JOE.

JOE. Sorry, you were saying?

GABBY. We're low on Frasers already, Taj is labelling up what's left out back – **Hi, yes, we do, they are in this bay here and to the left here, they get taller as you go to your right. Okay –**

JOE. Has it been this busy all morning?

GABBY. It's been steady, yeah – **Hello, you okay there? Yes we do, no problem. Do you need a hand with those? Okay, no worries** – Do you know anything about the clutter under the hut? Piles of trunk ends?

JOE. Yeah they're mine.

GABBY. Don't tell me, you're going to make them into coasters?

JOE. Yeah, I thought /

GABBY. You won't make them into coasters. And what's that
pile of crap at the back of the cabin, the wires and stuff?

JOE. I was fixing that set of broken lights that woman brought
back.

GABBY. What for?

JOE. They're broken.

GABBY. We can't sell them.

GABBY *checks her phone.*

That's twenty minutes.

JOE. She hasn't called?

GABBY. She probably thinks calling in yesterday covers her for
the weekend.

JOE. Give her another five minutes, maybe she thought it was
half-past.

GABBY. I'll be busy again in five minutes.

JOE. She could still be unwell.

GABBY. Yes. And Maz might help me with the stocktake
tomorrow.

JOE. Is she around?

GABBY. In with the potted spruces last I checked. She's got
some fucking nerve, I tell you.

BETTY *arrives.*

JOE. Betty! We were just talking about you.

GABBY. Are you feeling better?

BETTY. What?

JOE. You were ill / yesterday.

BETTY. Oh, that. Can I leave my coat somewhere?

JOE. In the cabin.

GABBY. Are you? Feeling better?

BETTY. To be honest, I'm pretty much the same but sometimes you have to solider on, don't you?

BETTY *goes to hang her coat up.*

GABBY. She's got today.

JOE. What?

GABBY. If she's shit by dinner time you'll have to fire her.

JOE. I'm not –

GABBY. **Hello! Hi there, that's a lovely gun! Thank you! I'm dead. Do you need any help at all? Great, well, give one of us a shout.**

It's the assistant manager's job to discipline staff.

JOE. You'd love that wouldn't you?

GABBY. I'm not in to *Fifty Shades* but whatever you do in your spare time / is none of my business.

JOE. God, you've a properly filthy /

GABBY. **Hello, madam – I can give you the number of someone who can deliver for you.**

JOE. **No, not me I'm afraid.**

GABBY. **Yes, all day every day. Lucky me.**

JOE. **I can always give you a hand getting it in the car, sure? No problem, that's my pleasure, madam.**

GABBY. **Just needs some brute force I expect.** You're blushing.

JOE. I'm not firing Betty.

GABBY. She's nearly half an hour late, she wasn't here yesterday.

JOE. She was ill.

GABBY. She cannot be this useless. **Hi there, the plain wreaths are ten pounds –** You think this is busy now? – **the**

decorated ones are fifteen pounds – This is nothing – **the prices are all up on the board just here, right behind me** – Wait until next weekend – **My pleasure** – We need someone who is going to work hard.

JOE. You can't decide to fire her before she has even started – **I'm sorry, we don't have a toilet, try the pub across the road.**

GABBY. **Bye now.**

GABBY *checks her phone.*

I'm not having deadweight.

JOE. And a 'Merry Christmas' to you too, Mr Scrooge.

GABBY. Taj! Watch out for Maz in the four-foot rack. I had you down for a Grinch man not Dickens.

JOE. *Muppets Christmas Carol.*

TAJ *runs over to them.*

TAJ. Thanks.

GABBY. What?

TAJ. For the warning.

GABBY. No, go back and stop the kids from playing in them.

TAJ. Oh. Okay.

TAJ *goes.*

GABBY. I'm going to throw those bits of trunk out.

JOE. I'm making Christmas presents from them.

GABBY. You won't. We all do it, we all thought in our first year, we'll make coasters from the slices of trunk that we take off for people but you won't. It will take ages, you have to go out buy the varnish, the tools, you'd never get them even, they'll just sit under your bed for years.

JOE. I don't mind it taking a while.

GABBY. Just buy some from Ikea.

JOE. Don't throw them out.

GABBY. Fine. Hear me saying I told you so when you /

    BETTY *is back*.

BETTY. Da-dah! I could only find extra-large.

GABBY. There is only extra-large.

BETTY. I'll do better for you in a small.

GABBY. There is only extra-large.

BETTY. Just saying. **Hi there! Welcome to Festive Pines, have you bought a tree from us before? Well, all our trees are premium trees, all are non-drop and as long as you water them, they will all last you to January. We have three types of tree; firs, pines and spruces. Which of those do you like the look of best? Yeah, I know they're my favourite too. We price by height in feet, traditional, all the prices are up on the cabin there and around the site in various places, how high were you thinking? About my height? Well, I'm five foot seven, which just qualifies me for supermodel, so you want to be in the six-foot racks to your left, third and fourth bays along. I'll leave you to have a rummage through, feel free to pull the trees out and take a look at them, I'll come and catch up with you in a minute. My pleasure, have fun. Hi there, have you decided on that one, it's a real beauty, great choice. Do you need a stand and lights too? You'll want two hundred for that one, we have multicoloured and white LEDs, they're really great value, we've had ours for five years and they're still going strong. No, you leave that to us, we'll net it up for you and I'll take your payment through in here. Yes, of course, card's fine –**

    BETTY *goes*.

    JOE *smiles*.

GABBY. People are waiting at the netter.

    JOE *goes to net the tree,* TAJ *comes back over*.

TAJ. I need better music now. What?

GABBY. Betty is brilliant.

TAJ. At what?

GABBY. At selling trees.

TAJ. What is there to be brilliant about? They drive in to buy a tree and we have lots of trees. Does she sell them two?

Sorry I don't work here.

GABBY *is checking her phone again.*

GABBY. Taj.

TAJ. **Fine, yes, what? No we don't have anything cheaper, go to the guys on the corner. You're welcome.** Honestly, some people. No phones allowed.

GABBY. Just put whatever you want on. Just for half an hour.

TAJ *goes in.*

Hi, welcome to Festive Pines, do you know what you're looking for? Yes, we've got a few of those. Ha ha. Any particular type of Christmas tree? – A cheap one, of course, the cheapest start just here they get more expensive as you move up the hill. Yes, those prices are by height, not girth. Gosh, Jimmy Carr had better watch his back, hadn't he? My pleasure.

TAJ *comes back.*

TAJ. Betty is putting on Michael Bublé.

GABBY. **Ask one of the lads if you need a hand.**

TAJ. **Not me.**

GABBY. **Have fun.**

TAJ. You banned Michael Bublé.

GABBY. I banned Cliff Richard.

TAJ. Innocent until proven guilty.

GABBY. We know he made 'Mistletoe and Wine'.

TAJ. 'Feliz Navidad' is a crime against humanity and it will be in my head until May.

GABBY. Don't exaggerate.

TAJ. Again.

BETTY *comes back*.

BETTY. **I will definitely come by to try them with mascarpone, they sound heavenly, thank you. See you soon, take care now, bye.** What a lovely couple.

GABBY. Are you taking the piss?

BETTY. What?

TAJ. Please can we negotiate some alternative music?

BETTY. This is so much fun!

GABBY. I'm so pleased you're enjoying it.

TAJ. I'm usually allowed some good music.

BETTY. What time is it?

GABBY. Twenty-five to two.

BETTY. To two o'clock?

GABBY. Yeah.

BETTY. What time did I get here?

GABBY. Half-past.

BETTY. That's five minutes.

GABBY. Yes.

BETTY. It can't have been only five minutes.

TAJ. The thing is, Betty, some of us have highly intelligent, complicated brains and Michael Bublé unpicks circuits that might otherwise be good for, I don't know, saving humanity.

BETTY. **Wow! You look so pretty! An ice princess! Isn't she the most beautiful princess, Gabby?**

GABBY. **Were the outfits for aeronautical engineer and Chief Commissioner still out of stock?**

BETTY. **She is a very funny lady. Where are your mummy and daddy?**

TAJ. We must stop this now, it's already gone too far.

GABBY. **And what does your princess like doing exactly? Opening hospitals, clubbing in Chelsea? Oh. Freezing things until they die. Lovely. Let's go find your mum and dad and let these two sort this out between themselves like grown-ups.**

GABBY *leaves with the princess.*

BETTY. What's the matter?

TAJ. I can't bear Michael Bublé.

BETTY. Don't be silly, everyone likes Michael Bublé, he's Canadian.

TAJ. No, you don't understand, I will listen to it and sing along and be lulled into a false sense of bonhomie and festive spirit but I will wake up in January to find parts of my brain have died. **Up there.**

BETTY. **Just up on the left there, sir, third row along.**

TAJ. **Bye.**

BETTY. I don't understand.

TAJ. I think. I'm trying to think back there with the trees whilst I'm tagging. It's mindless so I try to think about things.

BETTY. What things?

TAJ. Research, my PhD – **Can you please ask someone else we're in the middle of a very important /**

BETTY. **They all carry a lovely scent but my favourite is the blue spruce.**

TAJ. I am trying to talk to you.

BETTY. What's your PhD?

TAJ. It's in biomedical science, it won't / mean anything to you.

BETTY. Don't patronise me, Taj, I know people at Leeds doing medicine.

TAJ. Incorporation of $\alpha v \beta 6$ targeting peptide into novel, low-seroprevalence adenoviruses and their evaluation as vectors for oncological virotherapy applications.

BETTY. What if it's not the Christmas album?

TAJ. No.

BETTY. 'Crazy Love' or /

TAJ. It's too late now, I've heard it.

BETTY. How is rock better?

TAJ. I don't know, it just is.

BETTY. Wow. You're really smart then.

TAJ. It's just – I'm sure you're just as – it's just different, specialist. You're very good with – you seem to really know how to speak to people. You're very good at this.

BETTY. Thank you.

TAJ. And very pretty.

GABBY *enters*.

GABBY. She was a proper little c–

BETTY. **Hello, welcome to Festive Pines. I am new, yes, how can you tell?**

GABBY. Joe is being a climbing frame – **One go each in the lucky dip!**

BETTY. That is so beautiful.

GABBY. Did you reach a truce on the music?

BETTY. We're going to find some kind of compromise. Oh, Gabby, would you?

GABBY. What? Oh. **Hi, can I help?**

BETTY. Do you have an iPod?

GABBY. **We're getting another delivery this evening, they go really fast.**

TAJ. In a box from 2008 somewhere.

GABBY. **Sorry, we only have what we have now.**

BETTY. **I could choose one for you and put it to one side. What kind of space is it going into? Right, so you want**

something nice and slim at the bottom. Perfect, I'll pick you the best one we get on the delivery this evening and put it in some water for you.

GABBY. **I'm sorry, Betty is really new so she won't know that we don't reserve trees.**

BETTY. **That's okay if they pay for it now, though, isn't it, and then you can pick it up tomorrow or Monday. Otherwise I think you'll miss out again.**

GABBY. **Well...**

BETTY. **Great, come through and I'll charge you for a six-foot one, will you need a stand or lights?**

BETTY *goes.*

TAJ. Why isn't she the manager?

'Feliz Navidad' comes on inside.

GABBY. **Hello. You think you've seen a what, sorry? No, no, that's our pet mole, isn't it, Taj?**

TAJ. **Yeah, that's Ratty. Mole.** Shit. See?

JOE *comes back over.*

JOE. Have we got any sharper knives?

GABBY. **That's four-foot, sir.**

BETTY *comes back.*

BETTY. **It will have a big label on it and I'll be here. My pleasure. Take care, bye!** Could we get some mince pies?

GABBY. No.

TAJ. This is like cryotherapy.

JOE. You couldn't cut custard with this.

GABBY. What?

JOE. I can't cut the net off the tree even.

BETTY. Okay, we won't have Michael Bublé.

TAJ. Or Jamie Cullum.

GABBY. **That's a five-foot one, sir.**

TAJ. Or the ginger one.

BETTY. That's enough, Taj.

GABBY. **The size is marked on the tag.**

JOE. What about headphones?

GABBY. **On all of them, that's right, that's a five-footer too, I think, there should be a mark on the tag.**

BETTY. Headphones!

GABBY. **That's it.**

JOE. When you're tagging out back.

GABBY. **Well done, sir, you're a –**

BETTY. Genius.

TAJ. Gabby won't let us have phones out.

BETTY. That's why I asked you about an iPod. I'll bring you mine tomorrow.

GABBY. **Got it? Super.**

TAJ. Am I allowed headphones?

GABBY. What?

TAJ. Joe suggested I have headphones so I can listen to whatever I want to out the back and tune this horror out?

BETTY. Isn't it a genius solution.

GABBY. Can I?

TAJ. What?

GABBY. Have headphones?

TAJ. No.

GABBY. There's your answer then.

TAJ. You are setting back science.

GABBY. Oh, shut up, Taj.

TAJ. Scrooge.

GABBY. I am the ghost of Christmas past, present and fucking future as far as you're concerned, Gonzo, so shut the fuck up and go tag trees.

TAJ goes.

BETTY. **Of course we can find you the perfect Christmas tree for the fairy! Have you had a go in the lucky dip? Amazing! What did you get? A chocolate! That's the best prize! Okay, ready, I've got your tiara. Let's go!**

BETTY goes.

JOE. What else is in there?

GABBY. It's a tin of Quality Street in sawdust.

GABBY's phone rings.

Yes? I can see it's y– Good afternoon and merry Christmas, this is Festive Pines: Gabby speaking. Yes. No. Yes. She's here today. She's fine.

Registering JOE's look.

She's very good. What? Okay.

She hangs up.

JOE. I thought we weren't allowed phones.

GABBY. For Sami to call.

JOE. Is that why you keep checking it?

GABBY. No.

JOE. Who are you waiting on a call from?

GABBY. No one. Ed.

GABBY's phone rings.

Good afternoon and merry Christmas, this is Festive Pines: Gabby speaking. I am cheerful. Honestly. A lady saw Maz this morning and we tried to say 'Careful of the mouse, madam' but she said – 'That is a fucking great rat' – It was hilarious. She said 'fucking' not me. Yes, can't wait, see you later.

BETTY comes back.

BETTY. This is such great fun, isn't it? I can't believe we get paid for this! What's the time now?

GABBY. Quarter to two.

BETTY. What? When's dinner?

GABBY. Six.

BETTY. Great. **I will come and save you from the evil snow monster! Here I come!**

BETTY *goes*.

JOE. How long until you go out there?

GABBY. One-way flight booked for January 4th.

JOE. What's he doing out there?

GABBY. Working in a bar. Setting up as a graphic designer. He did German at uni. He went back out there, did an internship and loved it so – now he's there. Job prospects are better, he makes rent easily on bar work. Sounds like he's having a blast.

JOE. How long for?

GABBY. Indefinitely. **Yes, we take cards.**

JOE. **You don't have to have it netted, no, but you won't get it in the car as it is – or on your bike – I reckon, yeah.**

What does that mean?

GABBY. **Hi there – well, you have come to the right place, have you been here before, do you know how it works? You do buy a tree and stick it in the plastic thing, that's the magic and sparkle I'm looking for right there – We're here if you need us.**

It means he lives in Germany.

JOE. My girlfriend was still in Wales when I first came here.

GABBY. Oh? **They're all non-drop.** How long have you been together?

JOE. We broke up.

GABBY. That's a great story, Joe, thank you. **No, I wouldn't put it in front of the radiator.**

JOE. **Treat them like fresh-cut flowers, turn the radiator off, plenty of fresh water.** But you're going out there so you'll be fine.

GABBY. Yeah.

BETTY (*off*). Joe! Can you give me a hand with this twelve-footer?

GABBY. She told you that wouldn't get boring.

JOE. I'm not bored.

> JOE *goes*.

GABBY. Of course you're not. (*Imitates Betty. Unkindly.*) 'Oh Joe! You're so big and strong and I'm so weak and pretty! Please help me lift this enormous tree so I can touch the top of your lovely big arm every time you help.'

Ah! Maz!

> GABBY *turns her ankle in an attempt to avoid the rat* – JOE, BETTY *and* TAJ *run to find out why she is shouting*.

Argh! Jesus, fucking, fuck, fuck, fuck, fuck, fuck.

> *The others look at her, horrified.*

I've turned my fucking ankle avoiding that fucking rat. What?

> GABBY *sees the children and their parents standing around her.*

Hello. Welcome to Festive Pines.

JOE. **She's fine, everyone, just a twisted ankle, our sincere apologies for the colourful language.**

BETTY. **Come back next year!**

TAJ. Sami's going to kill you.

GABBY. Oh God.

JOE. Right, come on.

> *He picks her up.*

GABBY. What are you doing? Put me down.

JOE. Taking you inside to get it wrapped up.

GABBY. Put me down.

JOE. No.

BETTY. She doesn't want to be picked up.

TAJ. Shall I call Sami?

GABBY (*simultaneous*).

JOE (*simultaneous*). No.

TAJ. I just meant because she's hurt and might need help not so he can fire her.

BETTY. You just swooshed her up.

GABBY. You're embarrassing me.

JOE. You're hurt, badly, shut up.

GABBY. Am I?

BETTY. Like she is so light.

GABBY. I am light!

JOE. Betty, go after those customers that left, bring them back and smooth it over, Taj, get the first-aid kit.

BETTY. I don't know how anyone's supposed to smooth that –

JOE. Betty, you're so amazing at this, I really need your help.

BETTY. On it.

BETTY *and* TAJ *go*.

GABBY. Am I badly hurt?

JOE. No.

GABBY. Then why are you still picking me up?

JOE. You just screamed 'fuck' repeatedly in front of half a dozen children and their parents, I'm making a bigger scene.

GABBY. Shall I pretend to pass out?

JOE. Don't overplay it.

TAJ *re-enters with first-aid kit*.

TAJ. Here.

JOE. Thanks, help Betty, we won't be long.

> JOE *puts* GABBY *down.*

> Get your boot off.

GABBY. Ow.

JOE. Shut up.

GABBY. It hurts.

> BETTY *comes back over.*

BETTY. Can I give them a discount?

JOE (*simultaneous*). Yes.

GABBY (*simultaneous*). No.

BETTY. Maz!

> BETTY *tries to jump into* JOE*'s arms but* TAJ *gets there before her.*

TAJ. He's so strong.

BETTY. Taj!

GABBY. Give them twenty-five per cent – just go away.

> BETTY *and* TAJ *go.* JOE *holds* GABBY*'s ankle and bandages it, very well, throughout this next section.*

JOE. It's just twisted.

GABBY. How do you know?

JOE. It's not dislocated, I can feel it's not broken and it's not swelling around your tendons.

GABBY. Oh. Okay. It hurts.

JOE. Here, have one of these.

> JOE *hands her a pill from his pocket.*

> Don't look at me like that. It's a painkiller.

GABBY. It looks like a horse tranquilliser.

JOE. It's strong. Take half.

GABBY. Are these for your hand?

JOE. No, the weekend. Yes.

GABBY. Are you in a lot of pain?

JOE. Not when I take those I'm not.

GABBY. Ow.

JOE. Sorry.

GABBY. What did you do?

JOE. I put a glass through it.

GABBY. Ouch.

JOE. Yep.

Beat.

GABBY. Pint glass?

JOE. Yep.

Beat.

GABBY. When will it be better?

JOE. I've got my final ultrasound in a couple of weeks.

GABBY. Have you arranged the rota? Ow.

JOE. I'm already off.

GABBY. Then what?

JOE. Then I get a new contract and go back to training.

GABBY. Right.

JOE. How's that feel?

GABBY. Fine.

JOE. Too tight?

GABBY. No.

JOE. Want me to snap that in half?

GABBY. Are these why you're so cheerful all the time?

JOE. I don't take them any more.

GABBY. Does that mean you're in pain?

JOE. I'm fine. How does that feel?

GABBY. Much better. Thank you.

JOE. Don't put weight on it today, sit on the till, put it up on a chair. I'll send Taj out for frozen peas or something.

GABBY. I don't want to be on the till all day, I feel all cooped up.

JOE. You don't like the till, you whinge when you're labelling, taking a delivery, talking to customers.

GABBY. I don't whinge at customers.

JOE. You're rude to them.

GABBY. I'm not / rude.

JOE. You're sharp.

GABBY. You've only been doing this five minutes.

JOE. And it's not the worst job I've ever had.

GABBY. Yeah, as long as it's an in-between thing.

JOE. You'll be in Germany with Ed in, what, six weeks? And I'll be back on the pitch, so just try and enjoy it whilst you have to do it.

GABBY. And what if we're not?

JOE. Why wouldn't we be? – **Absolutely, madam, I'll be right with you** – You'll be all right.

GABBY. What makes you so sure?

JOE. I've seen dozens of these: you'll be walking on it again in a couple of days.

GABBY. Thank you.

JOE. We'll cope out here, unless you want to go home and not be paid?

GABBY. No.

JOE. Great. See you later then.

GABBY's phone rings. It is painful to get to it – either it's at a distance or it's in her back pocket and she has to stand to get to it. GABBY winces. JOE answers it.

GABBY. No wait, it might be.

JOE. It's not. Hi, Sami... She's turned her ankle... she's fine... bandaged up and on the till for the rest of the shift. It'll be sore for a couple of days but I've seen worse. I've got it, no worries, mate, see you later.

He hangs up.

I'm giving him a ringtone.

GABBY. Who? No, don't play with my phone.

JOE. Ed. I'm giving Ed his own ringtone so you know if it's him. Otherwise put this away and stop staring at it all day. I'll text Sami my number.

GABBY. Sami can still call me. Give my phone back.

JOE. No phones on site. There. Done.

GABBY. Wait, what is it?

JOE. You'll know when he rings, won't you.

BETTY *enters.*

BETTY. That was not easy.

JOE. My hero.

BETTY. Pick me up too.

JOE. What?

BETTY. Just – come on, it looked like fun.

JOE throws BETTY over his shoulder and she squeals with delight.

JOE. **Argh, oh no! I can't pick you up too, it's definitely against the law. Shall we put Betty in the netter?**

BETTY. No!

JOE. **Yes! In the netter!**

BETTY. **No! Joe!**

They exit.

GABBY *looks after them. A moment of watching the fun. Takes her pill, whole. Limps inside the cabin.*

'Song Three' – Taj

Scene Three

Sunday December 13th.

GABBY, JOE, BETTY *and* TAJ *are waving off the final customer. It is the end of the busiest weekend in mid-December. They are shattered.*

BETTY. **My pleasure, merry Christmas!**

And they are… gone! It's over!

JOE. That was insane.

BETTY. Where do they all come from?

GABBY. The week coming will be just as bad.

JOE. Everyone in the world bought a tree today, who's left?

BETTY. When that guy pulled up at two minutes to ten.

JOE. I nearly cried on him.

TAJ. Is this overtime?

GABBY. Talk to Sami.

JOE. Let's get out of here, who's got the energy for a drink?

BETTY. Awesome, same place?

JOE. Coming, Taj?

GABBY. Same place as when?

BETTY. I could murder a large glass of rosé.

TAJ. I'm having chips.

JOE. Would you like to come with us, Gabby?

BETTY *goes to pick something up and ends up sitting down next to it, she has no upper-body strength left at all.*

BETTY. I think my arms are gone.

GABBY. No, thanks, I need to stay for a bit.

JOE. What for?

BETTY. I ache. In here, down the side here, what muscle is that? Work is awful. Who knew?

GABBY. I have to do a stocktake.

JOE. Now?

BETTY. We don't have to, do we?

GABBY. It should have happened last night but the delivery was late and if I don't do it now we won't have the right trees this week.

BETTY. Give a shit.

JOE. Come with us.

BETTY. Does anyone else have this rash up the inside of their arms?

GABBY. It's okay, go.

BETTY. Dr Taj, have a look.

TAJ. I'm not a doctor.

JOE. A full stocktake?

BETTY. Yeah, you're medical though.

TAJ. It's a pine allergy.

GABBY. I'm quick.

BETTY. You are shitting me.

JOE. On your own?

GABBY. Just go, it's fine.

TAJ. Everyone gets it if you rub the sap against you too much, keep your sleeves down.

BETTY. I am allergic to pine, I can't do this any more.

TAJ. No, we've all got it, look.

GABBY. Just go, have fun.

BETTY. We are ALL ALLERGIC TO PINE!

JOE. God you're so.

BETTY. Oh thank God, I can show my dad this and he will let me stop.

TAJ. You like it.

BETTY. I do not.

JOE. Wait here five minutes, I'll be back.

BETTY. I thought we were going for a drink?

JOE. We are, five minutes.

   JOE *exits*.

TAJ. You look like you're having the time of your life.

BETTY. Look, when you're doing something, there's no point in being miserable about it, is there? But I'd rather be with my friends ice-skating and having cocktails and Christmas shopping.

TAJ. How do you know that's what they're doing?

BETTY. WhatsApp.

TAJ. That's mean.

GABBY. What are you still doing here?

BETTY. Waiting for Joe.

TAJ. You're not his type.

BETTY. Whose type?

TAJ. Joe's.

BETTY. What?

TAJ. He doesn't like high-maintenance women.

BETTY. What?

TAJ. He doesn't like high-/maintenance women.

BETTY. Okay – firstly, I'm not interested in Joe.

TAJ. Yeah right.

BETTY. I am not interested in Joe. I appreciate his physical
     form because I am not blind to beauty, but after my ex, I am
     done with rugby boys.

TAJ. What happened with your ex?

BETTY. It's like *every* Saturday? And two nights a week.
     Seriously?

TAJ. So you don't like sportsmen?

BETTY. This is the trouble, I am drawn to them, like, I really
     fancy them, but I know we are incompatible.

TAJ. Because you want them to be free on Saturdays.

BETTY. And now there are summer internationals and World
     Cup years, I mean, it's *endless*.

TAJ. So what is your type?

BETTY. I'm taking some time out right now to think about that.
     And just trying things out.

TAJ. Trying things out?

BETTY. Challenging my own preconceptions about people.

TAJ. Like what preconceptions?

BETTY. I think I should try and sleep with a black man.

GABBY. Fucking hell, Betty.

BETTY. I mean black as in the widest social and political
     definition. Not for the cock thing.

TAJ. So maybe, like, brown?

BETTY. Sure. I mean, why have I only ever got with white,
     middle-class boys?

GABBY. Seriously? You study sociology.

BETTY. I know, right?! It could be my dissertation.

TAJ. Great idea.

BETTY. Did Joe say he didn't like me?

TAJ. He was just saying his ex was high-maintenance and so I don't think he would want to go out with you.

BETTY. Who said anything about going out with him?

TAJ. I thought that's what –

BETTY. Ask him about me.

TAJ. No.

BETTY. Ask him if he likes me.

JOE *enters*.

TAJ. Joe, do you like Betty?

BETTY. Fucking – Taj is being such a dick.

TAJ. What's that?

JOE. Beers.

BETTY. I thought we were going for a drink?

JOE. This way we can have a drink, help Gabs with the stocktake and we'll all be done by eleven.

BETTY. What?

TAJ. Okay.

BETTY. I'm not staying to do a stocktake.

JOE. Come on, it'll be fun. Racks first?

TAJ. There's hardly anything left out back.

BETTY. Have you all gone mad?! It's home time, we have just worked the hardest day ever, let's go home.

JOE. It's fine, Betty, go.

BETTY. Everyone needs to go.

JOE. There's a stocktake that needs doing, so I'm staying to do it.

TAJ. Me too.

JOE. I got you wine.

BETTY. Red?

GABBY. I don't need your help.

JOE. No really, my pleasure.

BETTY. Worst. Sunday. Night. Ever.

JOE. You should stay off that ankle.

GABBY. You were right, it's better.

BETTY. Gabby, do you want wine?

GABBY. No.

JOE. Have a beer, cheer the fuck up.

BETTY. Whatever happens, do not let me drink seven hundred calories to myself.

TAJ. You helping or what?

BETTY. I'm just going to sit down for a bit.

GABBY. Betty, go home, it's fine.

BETTY. My friends went to a carol concert – look! All the candles! It's pretty.

GABBY. Go home.

BETTY. I'm hungry.

JOE. Eat the crisps.

BETTY. I'm not eating carbs right now.

GABBY. That must be very difficult to maintain.

    BETTY *inhales half the bag.*

JOE. Better?

    She nods.

TAJ. Is this really your first job ever?

BETTY. I'm only twenty-one, Taj, was I supposed to have been up a chimney?

TAJ. Most people have a job at school or uni.

BETTY. None of my friends had a job at school.

GABBY. I had a Saturday job at school.

JOE. Doing what?

GABBY. Bookshop.

BETTY. Obviously.

GABBY. You?

JOE. School until I was sixteen, then training academy.

BETTY. You haven't got any A levels?

JOE. Five GSCEs. A-star in Sports Science.

BETTY. You can't do anything without a degree these days.

JOE. What are you going to do with yours, Betty?

BETTY. Work for my dad. Probably.

TAJ. You should do this.

BETTY (*simultaneous*).

GABBY (*simultaneous*). Quiet in July.

JOE.

TAJ. You're amazing at it.

BETTY. I'm not working in retail.

TAJ. Why not?

BETTY. I have a degree, I will have a degree.

TAJ. Everyone has a degree, so what?

BETTY. Joe doesn't have a degree.

JOE. We can sing carols now if you like, Betty.

BETTY. Can you sing, Joe?

JOE. Good Welsh choirboy.

GABBY. Was your granddad down the mine too?

JOE. Paternal yes, maternal in the steelworks.

TAJ. I hate 'Away in a Manger'.

GABBY. It's a terrible carol.

TAJ. And the zoology is erroneous.

BETTY. What?

GABBY. I suspect you might be thinking about this too
    literally, Taj.

TAJ. At my school nativity, the kids could dress up as whatever
    animals they wanted. Cos it's multiculturalism innit. So
    around baby Jesus in the manger we had donkeys and sheep
    and cattle /

BETTY. That's in the carol cos they're lowing.

TAJ. And a camel.

BETTY. The wise men arrived on camels.

TAJ. And a Teenage Mutant Ninja Turtle, Spider-Man, three
    Transformers, a giraffe and, literally, half a dozen monkeys.

    Beat.

GABBY (*singing*). '*Away in a manger, no chimp for a bed –* '

BETTY. A game, a game! Put monkey into a carol!

GABBY (*singing*). '*Oh little chimp of Bethlehem –* '

    Beat.

BETTY (*singing*). '*Once in Royal David's City, stood a lowly –* '
    shit.

GABBY (*singing*). '*I saw three chimps come sailing in –* '

ALL (*singing*). '*On Christmas Day on Christmas Day –* '

JOE. Is there a line when this crosses into blasphemy?

GABBY. All right, choirboy.

TAJ. I'm an atheist.

BETTY. Are you allowed to be an atheist?

JOE. Can't we just sing them normally?

TAJ. What's your favourite carol then, Betty?

BETTY. 'The First Noel'.

JOE. Good choice.

GABBY (*singing*). '*The First Noel, the angels did say* – '

ALL (*singing*). '*Was to certain poor monkeys in fields as they lay* – '

BETTY. Can you play football?

JOE. No.

BETTY. Shame. What did you want to do, Gabby?

GABBY. What?

BETTY. When you left uni?

GABBY. I haven't – I still want to be a journalist.

BETTY. Have you thought about doing a Master's?

GABBY. I have one.

BETTY. Or an internship or work experience?

GABBY. I did three months, and then they offered me a job as a secretary and got another intern in.

BETTY. Going in as a secretary is a really good way to get in and work your way up.

GABBY. None of the boys are thinking about starting out as secretaries.

BETTY. Have you written a letter to the editor of the newspaper you most want to work at?

GABBY. Yes. I have. Thank you, Betty.

BETTY. My dad knows the editor of *The Spectator*, I think, I could get his name for you.

GABBY. Thanks, it's fine.

BETTY. I just think if you really want something /

GABBY. I have tried everything, Betty. Everything. Nothing works.

BETTY. Have you thought about starting your own blog?

GABBY. Oh yeah. I've thought about it. I've thought about going into a bar with quirky mismatching wooden furniture, ordering a latte in a jam jar, turning on my MacBook Air and writing about the hilarious trials and tribulations of being a young twenty-something making one mistake at a time with my kooky but hilarious friends, who all wear fabulous vintage clothes as we Instagram ourselves artfully smoking liquorice rollies on the steps of our five-storey Victorian mansion on Peckham Rye and play at being poor whilst our parents subsidise our astronomical London rent.

Then I go back to scouring the automated email from the jobsite until my eyes sting and wait for the phone to ring – desperate to see a withheld number because that's my temping agency asking me to sit behind another reception desk and stare into space all day for eight pounds an hour and listening to everyone telling me that I'm not working hard enough because this didn't happen to them, they could always pay their rent, it wasn't like this in their day and 'have you tried' – fuck – have you tried writing a letter to the editor?

I have given writing a blog some thought. Thank you.

JOE. You should write something. If you want to be a writer.

GABBY. You should play some rugby if you want to be a rugby player.

BETTY. It's so sad that you are so bitter.

GABBY. Has anyone ever called you a spoilt princess, Betty?

TAJ. I'm going to cure cancer.

JOE. Well done, Taj.

TAJ. Thank you, Joe, I'm going to get my PhD funding and then I'm going to have a wing named after me in a hospital somewhere.

JOE. Good luck, mate.

TAJ. My parents will then finally understand why I'm not going to be a dentist, I will marry a beautiful girl with a faraway sadness and spend my life trying to make her happy.

JOE. Here's to curing cancer.

TAJ. What's your favourite carol?

JOE. 'It Came Upon a Midnight Clear'.

GABBY. That's mine.

JOE. Sorry.

TAJ. I can go tag or I can go get more beer.

GABBY (*simultaneous*).

JOE (*simultaneous*). More beer.

TAJ. Shit I haven't got ID.

BETTY. Here, take mine.

    Beat.

    Oh yeah, okay, I'll come, I need chocolate.

    BETTY *and* TAJ *exit.*

JOE. She's only /

GABBY. I know. She just…

    Beat.

    You like her then?

JOE. She's sweet.

    Beat.

GABBY. When you were with your ex.

JOE. Cerys?

GABBY. The Welsh – yeah – how often did you call her?

JOE. Every day.

GABBY. Right.

JOE. Hasn't he taken full advantage of that ringtone?

GABBY. What is it?

JOE. What?

GABBY. The ringtone.

    Beat.

Doesn't matter, he's busy or – boys don't call, right, it doesn't mean anything. I mean, you called, but you're… So.

JOE. We broke up, Gabby.

GABBY. Yeah.

JOE. So it's probably not a good example.

GABBY. No.

Beat.

If you hadn't called her in nearly a month though, that would have been bad.

JOE. Yeah.

GABBY. Okay. Good. I mean, not 'good', I'm just not going mad. That's one good thing at least.

Beat.

JOE. Has he said anything?

GABBY. Like?

JOE. 'I need some space' or –

GABBY. No. No, he's not said anything. At all. Since Wednesday November 18th.

JOE. It'll be all right, Gabby.

TAJ *and* BETTY *enter.*

BETTY. I work in a shop!

GABBY. What?

BETTY. The guy at the offie said, 'Oh you're the Christmas-tree-shop people' and Taj just agreed with him.

TAJ. We are.

JOE. There's nothing wrong with working in a shop, Betty.

BETTY. I'm a student!

TAJ. We get change from him all the time, we're wearing our fleeces.

BETTY. I hate Christmas!

JOE. No you don't.

GABBY. Are you religious, Joe, is that it?

BETTY. They should tell you, the best one is when you are four, you don't remember it properly, don't try, John Lewis cannot sell it to you again, it's over.

JOE. Is that what – ?

BETTY. All these kids coming in here, bright-eyed and hopeful, everyone looking forward to this day that is always just the hugest anti-climax.

JOE. Christmas is – it's not about selling trees, is it? Come on, you don't mean any of that.

GABBY. Is that why you don't like the monkey-carol game?

TAJ. Are we doing 'true meaning of Christmas' stuff now, because I have to say as an atheist brought up with a Muslim cultural heritage /

JOE. The looking-forward is the best bit. The hope.

GABBY. It's delusional.

JOE. You feel happy, though, don't you? So Christmas Day can be a bit crap but for three weeks, you feel happy. Now is the best bit: everything still to look forward to!

GABBY. What am I looking forward to?

TAJ. Berlin.

BETTY. Actually, Joe, I am looking forward to this Christmas Day because I'm going to stay in bed until 4 p.m. and eat cheese until it comes out of my eyes.

JOE. You're not destitute or homeless or in the middle of a civil war / or fleeing your country, Gabby.

GABBY. That's not what I asked you: what have I got to look forward to? Actually there's a grotesque argument that someone fleeing Syria or South Sudan has more to look forward to than we do because their circumstances will almost certainly improve.

JOE. You're comparing doing a job you consider beneath you to being a Syrian refugee?

GABBY. No. I am asking you to qualify your baseless, unfounded, relentless optimism. How is everything going to be all right? Why is that your answer to everything? Because where you see stuff I have, I just see stuff that has gone horribly wrong or that will go horribly wrong very soon.

JOE. Then you need to shift how you're looking because it sounds like we're seeing the same thing.

GABBY. You cannot be seeing what I see because the next twenty years is terrifying.

BETTY. Twenty years? Christmas is in ten days.

TAJ. She doesn't think this job is beneath her.

GABBY. YES I FUCKING DO! Taj, it's beneath all of us.

BETTY. YES! We are all allergic to pine!

GABBY. I have a first-class honours degree and an MA with distinction and I'm counting trees for a living.

BETTY. Only for another couple of weeks.

GABBY. When our parents were our age they owned property. Imagine that! They had jobs for life, pensions, holidays, life insurance, nice cars.

JOE. My parents work in Morrisons.

BETTY. Both of them?

GABBY. Do you look at climate change and capitalism failing and the lack of natural resources to support ten billion people and just think: I'm sure it will be okay / no one will miss Norfolk that much anyway?

JOE. You're not making this about climate change.

TAJ. Technically, actually, it is something to look forward to. In a scientific sense not a... Christmassy sense.

BETTY. No one will miss Norfolk.

JOE. Climate change is what you're angry about, now, is it?

GABBY. Yes. Have you heard of it? It's a really bad thing that is definitely going to happen.

JOE. It's not what you're angry about, though. Is it? 'Capitalism failing'? It failed some of us a generation ago, you over-privileged, London-centric, middle-class, entitled crybaby.

GABBY. I grew up in Sussex. Actually.

JOE. I grew up in South-East Wales – which, just for the record, means I would rather lose all my limbs than play rugby for England –

BETTY. Then you probably wouldn't get selected if you'd lost *all* / your limbs.

JOE. Where as you correctly though disparagingly assumed, there *were* coalmines and steelworks and a life. And that life went. Wholly utterly and without warning or negotiation. And that wasn't fair either. My parents despaired of having children and the kind of life they would have and yet, here I am. We live on. We manage.

GABBY. I'm not talking about your parents or refugees.

JOE. Oh, now we're getting to it.

GABBY. Getting to what?

JOE. I was trying to give you some perspective, but go on.

GABBY. You're trying to tell me it doesn't hurt. It's all anyone does.

JOE. You're only as hurt and as frightened and as miserable as everyone else. You're angry because you were told that you were clever, special, entitled and you could do whatever you wanted to and it turns out you are just the same human being as the one clinging to a raft only far less well prepared. The world doesn't owe you a living.

BETTY. Wow. Wait, what?

JOE. 'You can do whatever you want to, darling, you're special.' Guess what? Everyone else's parents told them the same thing. And the reason you're really angry isn't that the planet is falling apart – I had heard, thank you – it's because the world isn't falling over itself at the great tragedy of you not meeting your bourgeois aspirations.

GABBY. Big word.

JOE. Sorry – stuck-up, conventional / materialistic.

GABBY. I know what it means, for fuck's sake.

JOE. No one cares if you're not a journalist, the world will keep turning.

GABBY. My mistake for thinking you might care, Joe. Sorry.

Beat.

BETTY. Everyone's being very negative.

TAJ. I care, Gabby.

GABBY. Can you all go home, please?

JOE. What about the stocktake?

GABBY. I don't want you here.

TAJ. I want to be here with you, Gabby.

GABBY. For God's sake, Taj, it's been three years, I was horribly drunk and it was a mistake. I never fancied you. Move on.

JOE. Yeah, okay, I'll go home.

BETTY. Hooray!

GABBY. Good.

JOE. You've got a nerve, calling her a spoilt princess.

BETTY. Yeah.

TAJ. She's very unhappy at the moment.

JOE. What gives her the right to talk to you like that just because she's unhappy?

TAJ. I do.

BETTY. You shouldn't.

GABBY. Oh, fuck off, Betty, you dumb, stuck-up bitch!

Pause.

TAJ. I think probably you should go actually, Gabs.

GABBY. *I'm* doing a stocktake, you guys just...

JOE. Stayed to keep you company and have a fun night?

GABBY. At least I have options, not four GCSEs and a train ticket to Newport.

JOE. Some of us have to get the Megabus.

GABBY. I least I still have a plan.

JOE. Do you?

TAJ. I think the best plan now, Gabby, is for you to go home.

GABBY. Fine. You lot finish the stocktake.

GABBY *collects her things whilst the others watch her in silence.*

I'll see you all tomorrow.

GABBY *exits.*

BETTY. Wow. What a bitch.

TAJ. That was awful.

JOE. Let's just get this done.

BETTY. Wait, we're *still doing the stocktake*?

TAJ. Shall I go after her?

JOE. Talk to her in the morning, Taj.

TAJ. That was the worst thing that's ever happened to me.

BETTY. I just don't think about all those things she was getting so angry about. I mean, now I have and I'm really depressed.

JOE. Okay. What's the worst thing you can think of? The worst thing that could happen or the worst thing that has happened?

BETTY. That's not going to make me feel better.

TAJ. Not getting my PhD funding.

BETTY. Okay – failing my degree – no – yes – failing my degree and having to work in Morrisons. No, it was in my head, sorry what's it called, Asda. No – Aldi.

TAJ. Are you going to tell us that there is always something worse than the thing we think of, so working in Aldi, you could always be working in Aldi and have one leg. I could always have no PhD funding and have cancer.

BETTY. Which would also be ironic. (*Hiccup.*)

TAJ. However bad things are, you can always imagine them to be worse.

JOE. No.

TAJ. Oh.

BETTY. I'm still in Aldi with one leg here.

JOE. I was going to say there is always hope. However bad things are, you can always believe they are going to get better. You can always choose to.

TAJ. Based on what?

JOE. What?

TAJ. Based on what empirical evidence?

JOE. It's not like that.

TAJ. Ah, well, as I explained, I'm an atheist.

JOE. It's not about God.

TAJ. You're saying you just have to believe. Have faith.

JOE. I'm saying you can't live like that. You can't live thinking things are always going to be as bad as you can imagine them to be, because that's like you're living with the worst-case scenario all the time. And even if all the evidence points to the world being pretty screwed, it's not there yet. Not yet. So why be miserable about it *now* when you could have been cheerful all that time until it really did get terrible? That's all I was saying. Fuck it.

Long pause.

BETTY (*singing*). '*Little monkey, little monkey, on the dusty road –* '

ALL (*quietly singing to finish the verse*). '*Got to keep on plodding onwards with your heavy load.*'

Smiles. Beat.

(*Very loud raucous singing.*) '*Ring out those bells tonight! Bethlehem! Bethlehem! Follow that chimp tonight! Bethlehem!*'

SAMI *enters at the height of the noise with* GABBY *close behind.*

SAMI. What the bloody hell is going on?

BETTY *screams.*

TAJ (*still singing*). '*Ring out those chimps tonight!*'

JOE. What are you doing here?

TAJ. Hello.

SAMI. I had complaints from the neighbours about the noise and the lights and Gabby told me there was some kind of party.

Beat.

What the fuck are you all doing?

JOE. We're stocktaking.

SAMI. Drunk?

JOE. No one's drunk.

BETTY *chooses this moment to throw up.*

TAJ. Betty's drunk.

SAMI. Get her off the premises.

JOE. Come on, Bets, let's get you home.

SAMI. Not you.

TAJ. Me? Okay. Okay. Great. Yeah, I'm taking Betty home, I'm going to take Betty home. I'm getting your bag. Sit there quietly.

SAMI. I'm waiting for some kind of explanation here.

JOE. A party?

GABBY. I –

SAMI. What are you doing on company premises after work hours, drinking, damaging stock and jeopardising my licence for next year?

JOE. Stocktaking.

BETTY *is sick again.*

BETTY. Oh God.

TAJ. I'm taking Betty home.

SAMI. Everyone's going home.

GABBY. I'll get the lights.

SAMI. Not you.

GABBY. Sam /

JOE. It's my fault.

SAMI. She's the manager: she's responsible.

GABBY. No, I mean yes: it's my fault.

BETTY. Oh God.

TAJ. Bye, everyone, see you tomorrow!

BETTY. Oh God, Taj, walk slower.

BETTY *and* TAJ *go.*

JOE. Sam, really, mate.

SAMI. Don't 'mate' me. You just screwed up big time. Our licences are temporary. If that neighbour had called the council we wouldn't get to be here again next year.

JOE. We were working.

SAMI. Sounded like it. Go home, Gabby, I'll deal with you in the morning.

GABBY. I was too tired to stay and stocktake, Sami, that's all, if I'd been here it never would have happened, it's my fault.

SAMI. Turn the lights off on the way out, please, Gabriella.

She leaves.

Pause.

I had plans for you. I wanted to give you some options come the new year. You're just another one with delusions of grandeur.

JOE. That's the last thing I /

SAMI. So much better than me.

JOE. This is just a misunderstanding, Sami.

SAMI. Sure. Good. Finish the stocktake tomorrow, come in at eight.

JOE. Thank you, Sami.

SAMI. What for?

JOE. Not firing me. I need the job, thank you.

SAMI. Course not. Someone has to clear that sick up. 'S all right, I'll wait.

JOE. What?

Beat.

We can put a hay bale on it or it'll rain.

SAMI. I said I'll wait.

JOE. There's no water on site or what am I /

SAMI. Loo roll. Tissue. Use your hands.

A beat. A stand-off. JOE *gets on his knees and cleans up* BETTY*'s vomit.*

GABBY *returns.*

GABBY. Sami, they were stocktaking.

GABBY *sees* JOE.

What – ?

SAMI. You need to start thinking about your future and all, Gabs.
I've got a meal ticket for someone and it isn't gonna be golden
balls down here any more. Get the lights. Go home.

JOE *continues, head down.* SAMI *watches. The floodlights
go out.*

'Song Four' – Gabby and Joe

GABBY*'s phone rings. It's Ed's ringtone: Slade – 'Merry
Xmas, Everybody'. She stares at it.*

Interval.

ACT TWO

'Song Five' – all

Scene One

Sunday December 20th.

TAJ *and* BETTY *are out the back, kissing.* BETTY *comes up for air.*

BETTY. Customer?

TAJ. Nope.

BETTY. Okay.

They carry on.

I cannot believe I'm snogging a scientist.

TAJ. It's amazing.

BETTY. Are you really going to cure cancer?

TAJ. It's a mathematical certainty. There are only so many options to try and we've tried a lot of them. Our techniques are getting faster, the methods are improving. If we didn't keep getting distracted.

BETTY. Sorry.

TAJ. No, by, like, major pandemics.

BETTY. Oh. Major what?

TAJ. Bird flu, Ebola, whatever's next. It's frustrating because what these things need is solid, focused, steady application of time, effort and resources. You can't just come along and say, 'Well, five thousand people are dying of this thing over

here now, so can we look at that for a minute?' But that's
what happens. Funding is fickle.

BETTY. You do something important.

TAJ. That's not why I do it.

BETTY. Why do you do it then?

TAJ. I'm good at it. I feel, I dunno, I feel important when I'm
doing it but I don't do it because I think it's worthy or /

BETTY. You love it. You do something you love. I want to do
that.

TAJ. What do you love doing then?

BETTY. I don't know. I haven't worked it out yet.

Beat.

But this is fun.

They kiss again.

TAJ. I'm not sure I love curing cancer.

BETTY. What?

TAJ. I mean, sure, it's probably a good thing, definitely a good
thing to do, it's just I think it's the thing that I *can* do. I'm
good at something and the funding is there so.

BETTY. So you're curing cancer because they're paying you to.

TAJ. No, the funding is fickle, like I said before, maybe next
year it will be something else, but the opportunity is there
now, so what I'm saying is: maybe it's not about finding
what you love, it's finding what you *can* do. The thing you're
good at. So what can you do?

BETTY. Nothing.

TAJ. Oh.

BETTY. How I am supposed to know? This is my first job.

TAJ. You're good at it.

BETTY. I can work for my dad.

TAJ. Do that then.

BETTY. I don't want to.

TAJ. Why not?

BETTY. I don't even know what he does. It's near Harvey Nichols, which is really handy, but whenever I ask, it just feels like he's brushing me off? He says it's boring.

TAJ. Financial services are boring.

BETTY. Are they? Why do people do them then?

TAJ. I hear the money's impressive.

BETTY. I have that. I mean, my dad has that, so. Maybe I don't have to do anything. I think I'd like to do something, though. I think I'd like to find the thing I'm good at.

TAJ. I know something you're already really good at.

BETTY. Yeah?

BETTY starts undoing TAJ's *jeans*.

TAJ. Oh God.

GABBY *enters*.

GABBY. Hi, gang! What's going on in here?

Silence.

Betty, can you come in a bit earlier tomorrow?

BETTY. –

GABBY. You're due to start at noon I think but I'd really love someone else here from ten.

BETTY *walks out*.

How long is she going to keep this up for?

TAJ. Please can you go too?

GABBY. It's been a week.

TAJ. Please just can you go away for a second?

GABBY. I've said I won't tell them. Don't be like this, please, I can't bear it if you start being shitty with me too.

TAJ. It's not that.

GABBY. What then? Oh my God, have you got a semi?

TAJ. It's pretty full-on actually.

GABBY. Taj! Look, I'm really pleased you're still talking to me, I am, but /

TAJ. It's not for you.

GABBY. Oh. Well, good.

TAJ. It's gone now anyway.

GABBY. Good.

> BETTY *enters. Beat.*

Can you just shake your head or nod or something?

BETTY. –

GABBY. Oh, for God's sake, this is so childish, you will have to speak to me eventually!

BETTY. –

GABBY. Fine. Don't come in early, I'd rather not have you here.

> *As she moves away,* GABBY *has a moment of realisation about* BETTY *and* TAJ.

TAJ. I think she knows about us.

BETTY. How?

TAJ. She's quite intuitive.

BETTY. Whatever, it's just Gabby.

TAJ. You said you wanted it secret.

BETTY. Yeah, from anyone who matters.

TAJ. If Gabby knows maybe we can tell Joe and /

BETTY. No one's speaking to her so who is she going to tell? Besides it's so much more fun when it's just between us.

TAJ. So when we get back to Leeds I'll move so I can have a double bed in my room.

BETTY. Why would you do that?

TAJ. I don't want to always stay at yours.

BETTY. Let's just take this one step at a time.

TAJ. We're back there in less than four weeks.

BETTY. I'm not sure how my friends would feel about me dating a post-grad, let alone a scientist!

TAJ. I love you.

BETTY. That's incredibly sweet of you.

TAJ. This is amazing.

BETTY. Let's be like Joe said and live in the moment, okay? My head is way too full of trying to plan the future already.

BETTY *kisses him.*

TAJ. I don't have to be a scientist.

BETTY. What?

BETTY*'s phone rings.*

TAJ. I can be whatever you want me to be.

BETTY (*into the phone*). Hi, Mum, I'm still at work, you okay? (*To* TAJ.) Sorry, I need to take this.

Beat.

TAJ. Oh. Okay. Sorry.

TAJ *steps away leaving* BETTY *to talk.* GABBY *and* JOE *enter.*

GABBY. Joe, if I let you go home early now can you come in a couple of hours earlier tomorrow?

JOE. No.

GABBY. Big Nick didn't make it here today so Sami is going to come tomorrow to 'judge' us and I'd really like to get the place looking immaculate.

JOE. No.

GABBY. We win a prize if we get it!

JOE. No.

GABBY. A cash prize!

JOE. I can't.

GABBY. Why not?

JOE. –

GABBY. Why can't you come in earlier?

JOE. Because I start at two tomorrow.

GABBY. And I'm asking you as your manager.

JOE. As my manager in this shit temporary job that you hate and you only do to make everyone else's lives a misery?

GABBY. That's not true – **Yes, the leader has broken on that one, but we measure to the crown, which is fine, so I can't give you a discount. There are lots more that are fine.**

JOE. Yeah, that's the vibe I'm getting.

BETTY *and* TAJ *are back serving.*

GABBY. If you talk to me again then I've got gossip.

JOE. I'm not interested – **Hello, sir, that sounds very much like the Fraser fir but I'm afraid we are all out of those this year.**

GABBY. **I think it was a better year for them last year, better growing conditions. Global warming. It's probably putting Eritrean farmers out too.**

JOE. **We've still got great Nordmann firs, they're our best sellers.**

BETTY. **We have absolutely beautiful trees still left, sir – Sure I'll show you what we've got, come with me.**

JOE. Ask Betty.

GABBY. I have. But as she's not speaking to me, at all, I have no idea if she's available or if she's agreed or what.

BETTY. Can you please ask Gabby if I can go home early?

JOE. Gabby, Betty needs to go home early, can she go instead of me?

GABBY. What does she need to go home early for?

BETTY. –

JOE. What do you need to go home early for? **Just five- and six-footers left now I'm afraid, they start to the left here. They're thirty-five pounds.**

BETTY. Tell her, my mum just called and she wants me to come home.

JOE. Her mum just /

GABBY. It's not school, Betty.

BETTY. Tell her – I think it's important.

JOE. She can go home early instead of me, can't she?

GABBY. Tell her /

JOE. **Just multicoloured ones left now.**

BETTY. **They're ever so pretty.**

GABBY. Tell her if she starts speaking to me again, she can go.

BETTY. Tell her – trust me she won't like what I have to say.

GABBY. I'll cope.

BETTY. Ask her how she'll know if I'm speaking to her or not if I'm not here because she sent me home.

JOE. How will you know /

GABBY. I heard her, Joe! Go home.

BETTY. Bye, Joe, see you tomorrow, I'll call you later, Taj.

BETTY *goes*.

TAJ. **Hello. They are all great. They all smell lovely, they all make you feel warm and Christmassy and just like life is suddenly everything you thought it could be, like the life**

**that happens to other people like – yeah, the ones we
have left for under forty pounds are over to the left there.
Cheers.**

GABBY. Does Taj seem different to you?

JOE. No.

GABBY. Are he and Betty having a thing?

JOE. None of my business.

GABBY. Please come in earlier to help me sort the site out
because I'd really like Sami to stop being horrible to us all and
give us 'Best Outlet'. And because we could win fifty pounds
and we could go to the pub together properly. I'd like that.

JOE. No.

GABBY. I can't say sorry any more times – **Hello, what?
Right. Right. I've never managed a tree in any of my
house-shares in London. Forty pounds? Well, the only
trees we have left are thirty-five pounds and the stands
are ten pounds and the lights are twelve pounds so you'll
have to go back to 'the boys' and get some more money
or see what the guy on the corner has left.**

The 'boys' have sent them?

JOE. **Excuse me, ladies? Hi, look, this one has a broken
leader, but it's a gorgeous tree, isn't it? So what I'll do is
make it a four-foot one, technically without the leader
that's what it is, you'll get away with a cheap stand if I
trim the trunk down for you, that's a fiver. There's a set of
lights in the cabin that someone brought back broken but I
think I've fixed them. I just can't sell them, if you promise
not to sue me if they trip your fuses then you can have
them. Thirty-nine all in. How's that? My pleasure, not at
all, we can't send you back empty-handed to the lads, can
we? Not at all, I'll find those lights. Tell Taj at the till that
Joe said it was a four-foot. Okay. Merry Christmas.**

Better get on the phone and tell Sami.

Beat.

I can't come in early tomorrow.

GABBY. Forget it.

JOE. I can't come in early tomorrow because I have to go to the hospital for my scan.

GABBY. It's tomorrow?

JOE. I'll come in when I'm done.

GABBY. Thank you.

TAJ. Are we discounting stock now?

GABBY. Let them have that one for four foot.

TAJ. I did.

JOE. I'll sort the trunk out and find those lights.

JOE *goes*.

Beat.

GABBY. So you and Betty /

TAJ. I'm sorry, Gabby. But it's serious. I love her.

GABBY. Wow. Okay.

TAJ. It's no use being sorry now, Gabby.

GABBY. I'm not /

TAJ. You had your chance.

GABBY. I appreciate that /

TAJ. We found love.

GABBY. Okay.

TAJ. Right where we are.

GABBY. Of course you did.

TAJ. I'm going to withdraw my PhD application.

GABBY. What? Why?

TAJ. She said she doesn't know how her friends would be with her dating a scientist.

GABBY. Betty said – wait, roll back, what's happened?

TAJ. We're in love.

GABBY. But she's worried about how her friends will feel about you? Is that love?

TAJ. Don't patronise me, I know how I feel.

GABBY. And you're sure you know how she feels?

TAJ. **I can take those branches at the bottom off for you.**

GABBY. **Just the multicoloured ones left.**

TAJ. Just because you don't want me doesn't mean no one else will.

GABBY. I didn't mean that, Taj, really I didn't.

The one on the left is a better shape.

It's a big decision to make for someone else, is all I meant.

TAJ. It's not *your* decision, it's mine, I don't want to be a research scientist, I want to be happy.

GABBY. Until last week that was – **Yes, the potted ones only come small, otherwise they would be too big for the pots** – That is what would have made you happy – **You *can* plant the big ones out but they'll just die –**

TAJ. No, it's what I was expected to do.

GABBY. No, your parents expected you to be a dentist and you didn't do that.

TAJ. **What is it, six foot? What you driving? Yeah, it'll fit, why else would you have a Vauxhall Astra?**

GABBY. Taj. Please. Listen to me. Don't withdraw your application. This is one of those moments where you are standing outside your friend's life watching them make a massive, massive mistake.

Yes, that's where all the six-foot ones are.

TAJ. Like we all felt when you didn't take that job after your internship? Everyone else said behind your back, 'She's crazy not to take it.'

GABBY. It was an admin job.

TAJ. Even Ed. Not me though. I said, 'She's better than being a secretary.' I supported you, I stood up for you.

GABBY. I didn't know any of that.

TAJ. Didn't you? When have I ever said, 'They told you so'? When have I ever pointed out that it was the best offer you've had in three years? You'd be there now, probably worked your way up a bit, probably showed them what you could do, working for a newspaper.

GABBY. As a secretary.

TAJ. You have to start somewhere, Gabby. But you're too proud to understand that. Too busy telling everyone what you should be doing and why you don't have what you're entitled to.

GABBY. You're doing it now. You're telling me so now.

TAJ. **Leave it by the netter, we'll sort it out.**

I can see the direction my life was heading in – lonely, single bed, researcher, hanging out with the geeks, spending my days trapped in a lab.

GABBY. You love your geeky friends.

TAJ. I don't have any friends, I have lab partners. I love her. She doesn't care about the future, she's living in the now and I want to live in the now. Now. So I'm gonna.

Yes, just this one, is it?

GABBY. Please don't withdraw your PhD application.

TAJ. Sorry, Gabs, I'm not staying behind being miserable on my own whilst you go to Berlin.

On my way, sir, apologies.

GABBY. Sleep on it at least.

TAJ. If I send the email tonight they might get it before the holidays, I'm seizing the moment!

JOE *returns*.

JOE. Taj, you okay cashing-up, I might split.

GABBY. I am here.

TAJ. Sure.

GABBY. Wait! Joe.

JOE. It's half an hour, it's quiet.

GABBY. Have you got someone to go with tomorrow?

JOE. What?

GABBY. To the hospital? Have you got someone to go with you?

JOE. What for?

GABBY. I dunno… to hold your hand?

Beat.

I could ask Sam to cover.

JOE. What about 'Best Outlet'?

GABBY. I'll lose for the fourth year running. I've coped without the recognition this long.

JOE. You like hospitals, is it?

GABBY. I care what happens to you.

JOE. All of a sudden.

GABBY. I'm sorry.

JOE. You've said. Will it make you feel less guilty if I let you come?

GABBY. Yes.

JOE. **Here, just coming!**

GABBY. What, you giving it away and carrying it home for them as well?

JOE. They're buying me a drink to say thank you.

GABBY. What, with their one-pound change?

JOE. No. Thank you. I'll be fine on my own.

GABBY. Okay. Go on then, have fun. See you tomorrow.

JOE. Night.

GABBY. Good luck.

JOE. Yep.

He goes.

TAJ. Go too if you like, I'm fine on my own.

'Song Six' – Betty

Scene Two

Monday December 21st.

8.50 a.m. BETTY *sits, crying.* GABBY *enters.*

GABBY. You came early! Thank you, Betty, thank you. You with Taj?

BETTY. Why does everyone think I'm marrying Taj? I just slept with him a couple of times, that's all, you can have him.

Beat.

GABBY. I meant are you with him right now? Is he here? Because he's supposed to be and you're not supposed to be.

BETTY. Oh. No.

GABBY. What's the matter, did you have a fight?

BETTY. No.

GABBY. Are you here to work the shift?

BETTY. My daddy got fired.

GABBY. Shit. What for?

BETTY. The police were at our house at 5 a.m. this morning to get him.

GABBY. God, Betty, what happened?

BETTY. He lied about owning some shares or not owning some shares or knowing about rates or something.

GABBY. *That's* your dad?

BETTY. What?

GABBY. He's all over the – I heard about it. I'm really sorry.

BETTY. My parents were screaming at each other right until he got put in the back of the police car. My mum's gone to live with my nan. In Eastbourne.

GABBY. Jesus, I'm so sorry.

BETTY. I don't want to live in Eastbourne.

GABBY. No, I can see that.

BETTY. Mum says they're going to repossess the house. What am I going to do?

GABBY. **Hi, I'm afraid we're not open just yet – It's only five to – Yeah – Actually we haven't set up yet so if you can just give us until we've – Please, just, less than five minutes – Because we open at nine.**

BETTY. **You can't look around because we're not fucking open yet, you moron, she's said it three times! Go and sit in your car until we turn the sign round!**

GABBY. **We'll just be a few minutes, really. Thanks.**

Beat.

Listen, you'll be fine, you're going to go back to uni and get a first /

BETTY. I can't get a first any more, I only got a 2:2 last year.

GABBY. And get a 2:1, which is great, and then you're going to do whatever you want to do. It's your future, Bets, not his.

BETTY. I've got credit cards with nearly twenty-five thousand pounds on them.

GABBY. Wow.

BETTY. Yeah.

GABBY. That's /

BETTY. Yeah.

GABBY. How did you spend twenty-five thousand pounds? You live in Leeds!

BETTY. The shopping is excellent.

Beat.

They made him wear handcuffs. It's Christmas.

TAJ *enters*.

TAJ. Morning, ladies.

BETTY. Good morning!

GABBY. Hi, Taj.

TAJ. You're not in until twelve.

BETTY. My night got out of hand! So I have decided to plough on through.

TAJ. You went out like that?

BETTY. Yes I did.

TAJ. Was your mum okay?

BETTY. Fine.

GABBY. Really?

BETTY. Absolutely.

Beat.

GABBY. Get yourself some breakfast from the café and come back.

BETTY. Dirty fry-up! Good plan, m'lady. They do great eggs Benedict at that one on the corner.

TAJ. You're never going to make it through a full day.

BETTY. Wanna bet? See you in a couple of hours.

Beat.

Oh my God, Taj, I am clean out of cash and the nearest /

GABBY. Here.

GABBY *takes a note from her back pocket and gives it to* BETTY.

Get us all tea on the way back with the change. Make sure there is change.

BETTY. Yes, ma'am.

BETTY *goes*.

TAJ. She's talking to you?

GABBY. Did you send the email?

TAJ. She has made me happier than I have ever felt in my whole life.

GABBY. **Hi, sorry, we had a small personnel issue.**

TAJ. You can open when I'm four minutes late.

GABBY. No, that wasn't – **Okay – Go to the guys on the corner, of course, sorry about that –** It wasn't you.

TAJ. Anyway it's done now so there's no point going on at me about it.

GABBY. What is?

TAJ. Written and sent last night.

GABBY. Oh, fucking hell, Taj.

TAJ. **Hi there, yes, tons of five-footers and more due on the delivery later today, come on in.**

GABBY. **Hi, no just the undecorated wreaths now. I don't know where else sells them –**

Can you get it back?

TAJ. What?

GABBY. **We might get some more on the delivery, it's due any minute actually.**

The email!

TAJ. Let it go, Gabby, I have – **Yes, this way, if you'd like to follow me.**

TAJ *exits*.

GABBY. **Always this busy in the last few days! Yeah, the leader is a bit bent on that one. I'll do it with five pounds off – you can just stick the star on it and no one will notice. Or you can keep looking. Thanks.**

SAMI *enters*.

SAMI. Morning, team. Judging day is here!

GABBY. Hooray! I'm so glad it's you and not Big Nick.

SAMI. What's going on?

GABBY. Nothing. We're really busy already and I had everything set up for Nick yesterday so – **Good morning! –** be kind.

SAMI. You carry on, my angel.

GABBY. **Lovely, let's get that netted up for you.**

SAMI. Aren't you a bit short-staffed?

GABBY. Betty starts at noon, Joe's in after lunch.

SAMI. Who's responsible for that bit of rota mismanagement then?

GABBY. Like I said, we were expecting Nick yesterday.

SAMI. Place should be spotless twenty-four-seven, Gabs, not just for 'Best Outlet'.

GABBY. Yes. You hired anyone for that job yet.

SAMI. You interested now?

GABBY. I might be.

SAMI. What happened to Germany?

GABBY. I'm not going.

SAMI. Do I need to have a word with him?

GABBY. What? No. That's – no. Thank you. It's fine.

SAMI. So you want to work for me now?

GABBY. I'm sorry if I gave you the impression that wasn't what I – I really enjoy this job. You know that. It's just been a funny few weeks.

SAMI. All right. I'll think about it.

GABBY. Thank you.

SAMI. I might roll my sleeves up and get stuck in here for old time's sake.

BETTY *enters with a large box.*

BETTY. I bought panettone!

GABBY. Where's the tea?

BETTY. It's such a good one.

GABBY. Betty?

BETTY. Where I am supposed to get four teas and breakfast for ten pounds?

GABBY. Stav's Caff does a Full English for five ninety-five including tea and three takeaway teas would have been three ninety. I should have fifteen pence change and a cup of tea in my hand.

BETTY. Stav's – what, that place on the corner with the fruit machine?

GABBY. Where did you think I meant you to go?

BETTY. The deli! Why would I think of going in that place?

GABBY. Because you can get breakfast and three teas to take away for ten pounds.

BETTY. I can't go in a place like that. You might be able to, but I can't.

GABBY. That was my last ten pounds!

BETTY. Hello, Sami! I bought panettone for everyone.

SAMI. Aren't you a love?

GABBY. Great, are you both just going to be in the way all morning?

BETTY. Will you pay me for the extra two hours if I start now?

SAMI. Sure.

BETTY. Super! Ten pounds for Gabby, panettone for everyone! You give it out.

She gives SAMI *the panettone and goes.*

SAMI. You said she was good, yeah?

GABBY. She's very good. She's also sleeping with Taj.

SAMI. She's what?

GABBY. You heard.

SAMI. Taj is getting some of that?

GABBY. Getting some of – that's disgust– **We are all out of mistletoe, I'm so sorry. Wreaths?** The wreaths are overpriced.

SAMI. Is it a freak fetish or something? **I'll do you that one for ten pounds, madam.**

GABBY. Stop discounting my stock.

SAMI. I'm shifting it, not going nowhere in January, / is it?

GABBY. Not going anywhere in January /

SAMI. Oh, shut up, Shakespeare.

BETTY *enters.*

GABBY. So it's full time?

SAMI. Depends if we get the sites we're after.

BETTY. Come on, Sami, you want a bit, Gabs?

GABBY. Yes.

BETTY. Full-time job, like all year?

SAMI. From June. We're branching out.

Silence.

West next year, pushing past Richmond into Twickenham and Surrey.

GABBY. Betty, that women needs help over there.

SAMI. TAJ! Don't let the lady struggle. We've got our hands full of cake stuff here.

BETTY. I'm your girl.

GABBY. I'm not sure you're the right /

BETTY. I'm the best here.

GABBY. It's lots of lifting, outdoors work.

BETTY. Everyone will tell you, I'm the best here.

SAMI. It's different to this, though. It's mud and farms and farmers and lorry drivers.

BETTY. Customers, contracts and charm. What farmer isn't going to love me?

SAMI. You serious?

BETTY. What's the money like?

SAMI. You start on fifteen K and then you get a bonus on sales.

BETTY. What bonus?

SAMI. Five per cent.

BETTY. Turnover?

SAMI. Sales.

BETTY. Net or gross.

SAMI. Gross.

BETTY. What were sales last year?

SAMI. Just over a million.

GABBY. Fuck me – **No, I can't give you a discount for a missing branch.**

BETTY. What's the percentage forecast for next year?

SAMI. Four new sites, increased sales of twenty-five per cent.

BETTY. I'm good at this, Sami. Watch me.

SAMI. I'm watching.

BETTY *moves off,* TAJ *enters.*

GABBY. Taj, what's five per cent of a million and two hundred and fifty thousand?

TAJ. Sixty-two thousand, five hundred. Why?

GABBY. You earn over sixty grand a year?

SAMI. Don't be daft. I'm on seven per cent.

GABBY. Are you seriously thinking of giving it to her?

SAMI. She good?

TAJ. She's brilliant. She really loves it; the people, the sales, she kind of lights up when she's here.

SAMI. That right?

GABBY. Yes.

BETTY. **See, when you cut the bottom of this tree like this, you can see how old it is by counting the rings, see here? Your tree is six years old. How old are you? This tree is older than you. That's how long ago we started talking to our farmer about this tree. When you put this tree in your living room you can look at it and think, 'Our tree was waiting in the field for six Christmases already before we came and picked it, waiting to be our best Christmas tree yet' – No you can't have it next year too because now that it is out of the ground he won't live more than a few weeks, but when you put this one out in January, it will get turned into wood chips to help the other trees grow. Like the new one growing right now out there somewhere for next year and the one being planted this spring that might be your Christmas tree in six years' time when you will be eleven! Imagine that, being eleven? Time's a mind-blowing idea, isn't it?**

SAMI. You're very good.

BETTY. So you'll consider me for the job?

SAMI. Is there something going on with you and my cousin?

BETTY. Where did you hear that?

SAMI. Gabby told me.

BETTY. Did she? Nothing serious.

SAMI. That's good to hear.

BETTY. Is that a yes then?

SAMI. Shall we talk about it over your lunch break?

BETTY. We only get half an hour. I was just going to eat the rest of the panettone out the back.

SAMI. See you out back later then?

BETTY. Sure.

'Song Seven' – all

Scene Three

A few hours later.

JOE *arrives*.

JOE. Sorry I'm late.

GABBY. It's nearly four. Big night, was it?

JOE. –

GABBY. With the girls?

JOE. Is Sami still here?

GABBY. Last seen hours ago with Betty re-enacting *The Lion King*. Where are you going? There's a queue at the till.

JOE *moves off to find* SAMI. BETTY *appears, adjusting clothing*.

BETTY. Wow. Crazy day.

GABBY. Where have you been?

BETTY. Out back stocktaking. I'm just waiting for Sami.

GABBY. Where is he?

BETTY. He's driving me to Eastbourne.

GABBY. Why would he do that?

BETTY. Well, we're, you know – working together and stuff.

GABBY. Right. Congratulations.

BETTY. You'll be fine without me for the last few days, won't you?

GABBY. You owe me a tenner.

BETTY. I'll pay you back. Promise.

GABBY. Taj sent his university an email yesterday telling them to withdraw his funding application because he's in love with you and you don't see yourself with a scientist long term.

BETTY. What? That is ridiculous.

GABBY. You made him believe /

BETTY. I did no such thing. We've been seeing each other for a week. He did what? Oh God.

GABBY. And now you're fucking Sami?

BETTY. What?

GABBY. You vanish with him back there for / hours.

BETTY. Yeah. Well, I needed the job, didn't I?

GABBY. You are really good at this job, Betty. You didn't have to fuck him.

BETTY. No, you're right, I didn't. I did it because I wanted to.

GABBY. Did it really feel like that?

BETTY. You'll tell Taj for me, won't you, and say bye.

GABBY. Whoa, no.

BETTY. What?

GABBY. No way.

BETTY. Really? I would have thought you'd enjoy that. Bringing misery.

GABBY. I judged you the minute you walked in here. And I was absolutely right.

BETTY. Nice working with you, Gabby.

BETTY *exits*. SAMI *enters, closely followed by* JOE.

JOE. Sami! You off, mate?

SAMI. Yeah, getting that one home. All the best if I don't see you again.

JOE. I know I've not put myself in the best position for it, but I'm a hard worker and the others will tell you I've been a real asset here this month.

SAMI. You want a reference?

JOE. I was hoping I could get an advance.

SAMI. A what?

JOE. I need the money from this week – just a couple of hundred of it actually – before the end of the month.

SAMI. I can't pay it any faster cos of the bank holidays and stuff.

JOE. It's just I need it to get me and my stuff home.

SAMI. This, my friend, is when you call the bank of Mum and Dad.

JOE. They'd come and get me usually but they're in retail too and this week is the biggest one for them.

SAMI. I can't help you, mate, sorry.

JOE. Don't call me 'mate'.

SAMI. What?

JOE. We're not mates. Mates help each other out.

SAMI. You want a personal loan now?

JOE. I just need a couple of hundred quid.

SAMI. Can't you call your pals down at the rugby club? Johnny Wilkinson and Halfpint or whatever?

JOE. Or I could stay and do some work for you in January?

SAMI. January? You want to sell Christmas trees in January?

Sorry, we are down to five- and six-foot trees now, nothing bigger. What, that one on the sign? Yeah, we can sell you that one. You'll need Big Man Joe to get it down for you though – make use of those guns, Joe?

JOE. Sorting the sites out, returning stock, nothing?

SAMI. Tell you what, here's a tenner, get that twenty-footer down off the sign and on that bloke's car. Saves someone putting it through the chipper.

GABBY. **I'll be over in just two seconds.**

SAMI. Nearly forgot! Gabby!

GABBY. Sami?

SAMI. Runner-up mince pies by the till for you. Better luck next year. Merry Christmas!

SAMI *goes.* JOE *leaves to get the tree down.*

GABBY. Why is Joe pulling the sign down?

TAJ. That man asked for the big tree and Sami said Joe would get it down.

GABBY. It will need all of us – **Hi. Right, sorry, if they have it now, then – I can't really get involved, sorry** – Has he got a van?

TAJ. Who?

GABBY. The guy that wants the huge tree?

TAJ. Why would I know?

GABBY. **If you put it back in the rack then someone else is entitled to pick it up, that's just fair, isn't it?** Let's see how this guy's getting it home before we struggle getting it down, can we? **Hi, were you asking about the big – yes it's twenty foot – have you got a van or a roof rack? No, it's definitely not getting in the back of an Audi TT.**

Taj, go stop him from pulling the –

They stand and watch as JOE *tears apart the twenty-foot tree. Possibly the sign too.*

– place apart.

TAJ. Too late.

GABBY. I cannot tell them to give your tree back, because it's not your tree. You put it back in the rack which – There must be fifty other trees, please just choose another one, they're all lovely. Sorry, I need to help my colleague – We *had* a twenty-foot tree that would never have gotten into the back of your car – No, it's not your tree until it's tagged and paid for – Would you just both excuse me for –

JOE *enters, perhaps with bits of tree.*

JOE. I've got two ten-foot trees. Who wants one? I can probably tidy the base up with a saw for you. Or we have smaller ones, we've always had smaller ones, ones I didn't have to just cut down from the sign.

GABBY. I'm sorry, madam, you've done nothing wrong – Sir, please calm down, there are plenty of other trees.

JOE. North Face. Yeah, you. When was the last time you went up the North Face of anything? It's a tree, you sad fuck: choose another one. It's how you were speaking to them. Or do you mean – I can't speak to you like that because I'm picking on someone my own size. Well. Not quite – I'm not talking to you now. It's a very expensive, impressive car, you see, but it is only about twelve foot I reckon. So if you want a bigger tree than that, you probably need to come up here with a more practical car. Possibly one that doesn't scream, 'I'm a fucking wanker' – Can't I? Why not? You gonna do something about it? About me talking to you like this? What's up, you can dish it out to her, but I'm not allowed to give it back to you? Come on, you're wearing the kit, aren't you? You and North Face. Ready for anything. Aren't you? No? – You both gonna go away quietly and choose another tree then? – You are the customers not clients, that would be silly, I don't look or sound like someone who has clients, do I? Do I? I look like someone who breaks the faces of

public-schoolboy cunts for a living and by fuck I've missed it. Tell me again I can't speak to you like that. Go on. TELL ME AGAIN.

GABBY *steps in front of him.*

GABBY. Joe. Please.

JOE. **Take your fucking Gore-Tex and your piece of lying German-car crap and fuck off back to Dulwich.**

JOE *stares them off the premises. Then walks off.*

TAJ. He's the hulk.

GABBY. That's not helpful.

TAJ. That was the sexiest thing I've ever seen.

GABBY. –

TAJ. Wait till I tell Betty.

GABBY. **Hello, welcome to Festive – Yes, I'm sorry, please take that on us, madam, I really am very sorry. I really hope it hasn't ruined the entire holiday for you – your husband is – yes – I'm sorry. Really. It's not very Christmassy, no. I can see that. Of course you can complain, here, take this number and call our manager Sami... actually take this one and call Nicholas the owner. It's escalated beyond Sami, I think, don't you? His name is Gabs. My name is Jo. I'm the assistant manager here. I'm really very sorry, he's had some bad news. It's been a rough day. Would he like a go in the lucky dip? – no – that's fine – Gosh. Kids are like parrots at that age, aren't they? Sorry again. Thank you. Bye now.**

TAJ. Why are you pretending to be called Jo?

GABBY. What are you still doing here?

TAJ. I was waiting for Betty.

GABBY. Right. Sami is driving Betty to Eastbourne to be with her family because her dad is the guy in the news who has been arrested for fraud. **Hi there, welcome to Festive Pines.**

TAJ. What news?

GABBY. Her dad has been arrested for fraud. He's been fired. They have frozen his assets. They are repossessing their home and Betty has credit-card bills of twenty-five thousand pounds to pay.

TAJ. What's that got to do with Sami? Or Eastbourne?

GABBY. **No Frasers left, I'm sorry, just Nordmanns now, I'll give you a hand in a sec.** It's to do with Sami because she is going to take the full-time job with him and because she just shagged him out the back. Eastbourne's irrelevant.

TAJ. Are you making this up?

GABBY. She asked me to say goodbye to you.

TAJ. You just want everyone to be as miserable as you are.

GABBY. I don't.

TAJ. Yeah you do, you always did. Well, now we all are. You're like the poison ivy of Christmas.

GABBY. That's not a very traditional decoration.

TAJ. This used to be such a fun job! You used to be so great, so funny, we used to have such a great time! What happened to you? I'm going home now.

GABBY. See you tomorrow.

TAJ *exits*.

You okay there? Me? I'm fine. Bit tired. Yeah, it has been. Thank you so much for asking.

JOE *enters*.

JOE. Go on then.

GABBY. Hello. Go on then what?

JOE. Fire me.

GABBY. **See that's a Christmas tree. The Fraser you wanted, their branches are way too tight to decorate properly, they look stunning here, but once you get the lights and all the other stuff on it, it looks a bit angry.**

**These guys, they have big spaces between the branches,
so they look a bit gappy and sad here, which is why we
have more left, but those of us who have been doing this a
few years, we know that these trees were born to wear
tinsel. They need you, they need some TLC and they will
reward your attention and kindness. Great choice. Let's
ring her up for you.**

GABBY *goes into the cabin leaving* JOE *alone for a
moment. There is music. There are lights. He might cry.*
GABBY *comes back out with a box.*

Thanks. Merry Christmas.

Loser mince pie?

JOE. Thanks.

They eat. Beat.

GABBY. What happened?

JOE. It's a severed tendon. The glass severed a tendon. Tendons
don't heal. I've lost mobility in my hand for good, see? I
can't bend my middle finger all the way?

GABBY. That's hardly anything.

JOE. You ever managed to catch a rugby ball?

GABBY. No, they're so awkward. Right.

JOE. They told me in November: ninety per cent it was
finished. I heard: ten per cent it's fine. I've spent every penny
I have on more tests, more scans, more exercises, more
physio. It didn't hurt any more so I couldn't understand why
it wouldn't be better.

GABBY. I can lend you two hundred pounds.

JOE. I can't take that from you.

GABBY. It's just sitting there. I had it saved for Berlin. So.
Nice ringtone by the way.

JOE. What did he say?

GABBY. He didn't really. He stopped speaking to me for a
month and then he called to let me do it.

JOE. That's a really shit thing for him to do.

GABBY. Yes it was. Thank you.

Beat.

You want to know why I hate that song?

JOE. Which / one?

GABBY. Your ringtone for Ed. Slade.

JOE. Seems obvious.

GABBY. They always played it on the last day of term at my school. Pantomime, then Slade, then final assembly. There's a line that goes (*Sings.*) '*Look to the future now, it's only just begun –* ' Whenever I hear that line now something catches in my chest like a – sob. You're right. Us lot that grew up in the towns with the Aga showrooms and the coffee shops: we were all told that we deserved something better. We *all* went to uni. Not all of us can be that bright. We've all been told we have something bigger to say or be, we're all the Leaders of Tomorrow. What if we're not? What if we don't? A girl from my MA has a weekend magazine column. One thousand words every week to stitch over the gaping chasm of vapidity between Emily Davison and the virtues of a good lipgloss. I feel like I'm stuck behind double-glazing watching everyone I know and love have the time of their lives.

Beat.

JOE. My friends from school work in the chicken factory.

GABBY. Perspective-ometer as ever, thanks, Joe.

JOE. Or the UHT-milk factory or the high achievers work in the biscuit factory. Or they're on Jobseeker's. (*Re: mince pies.*) Are we finishing these?

GABBY. Fuck yeah.

Beat.

JOE. Tell a lie, some are in HMP Parc.

GABBY. Take the two hundred pounds, Joe, it's just money.

JOE. No. Thank you. I'll call my pa. He'll come get me. I have to tell him some time. I vowed I'd never go back unless it was in a red shirt on an open-top bus with streamers and a big cup. Everyone rushing out of the workman's hall to meet us, Ma and Pa crying with pride, lots of singing, the new sign with our name on the rugby club door, buffed and polished. Finally something for those people clinging to the side of the mountain to find some joy and some pride in.

You know I'm the first person in as many generations as they've done the family tree for to leave. Since 1600-and-something my family's been in the same four valleys.

GABBY. My dad's doing that, the family tree.

JOE. Ours is boring as shite.

GABBY. Sounds like it.

Beat.

Is that how your dad weighs up your worth then? Trophies and cups you brought home?

JOE. No. Never.

GABBY. Maybe we're not rugby players and journalists and graphic designers and oncologists. Maybe we're just daughters and brothers and sisters and sons and friends. No man's life is a failure if they have friends.

Beat.

That's from a film: *It's a / Wonderful Life*.

JOE. *It's a Wonderful Life*, I know.

GABBY. They haven't done a muppet version yet so I wasn't sure if it had hit your cultural radar.

Pause.

What you gonna do?

JOE. Go home. No other plan.

GABBY. You found the thing that made your soul vibrate. And you did it.

JOE. You've a lovely way with words.

It's dark. There are no customers. JOE flexes his injured hand.

GABBY. Does it hurt?

JOE nods and continues to hold it, flex it. GABBY reaches across and takes it. They hold hands.

'Song Eight' – all

Scene Four

Tuesday December 22nd.

SAMI *is lying on the floor, tightly wrapped in net. He struggles to get onto his feet. After several failed attempts he manages. As he stands, still wrapped up in net, GABBY enters.*

GABBY. Sami?

SAMI. Morning, Gabs. Bit of a misunderstanding with my cousin, that's all. Be an angel and cut me out.

GABBY. I thought you were in Eastbourne.

SAMI. Have you been?

GABBY. No.

SAMI. I came home.

GABBY. Have you been here all night?

SAMI. No. Yes. Since about five. You gonna cut me out then?

GABBY. I'd love to but all the knives here are as blunt as spoons.

SAMI. How do you cut the nets?

GABBY. With difficulty, it's a real pain. Health and safety innit. Wow, you're in what, three or.

SAMI. About seven layers I think.

GABBY. Wow. I mean you can just pull at them until they break, well, Joe can, but he's not here so I don't know what we're going to do. Well, I know what we should do first.

GABBY *gets her phone out.*

SAMI. Who you calling?

GABBY. No one, I'm just using the camera.

SAMI. Nah, come on, Gabs, babe.

GABBY. I'm not your angel, your sweetheart, your babe or your mate, Sam, and you have had this coming to you.

SAMI. What's it worth?

GABBY. What do you mean?

SAMI. Get me out of this, yeah, no photos, no fuss, no telling anyone, and I'll owe you then, won't I?

GABBY. You have nothing I want.

SAMI. You still after that job?

GABBY. What, the job you gave to your girlfriend?

SAMI. My what?

GABBY. Sorry, fuck-buddy or whatever.

SAMI. Betty?

GABBY. Yeah.

SAMI. I'm what? I'm not – I'm not sleeping with Betty. I've never slept with Betty.

GABBY. Yes you did, before she left, out the back.

SAMI. Behind the hut? That's – ! Who does that behind the hut? That's no way to do things.

GABBY. You were back there for hours.

SAMI. She was crying her face off back there for hours, going on and on about her dad and begging me not to tell Taj, I never – she was with Taj, I'd not do that to him. And we're gonna work together and she was born in 1994! It's illegal, isn't it?

GABBY. She said you did!

SAMI. We didn't! I swear.

GABBY. I told Taj you did.

SAMI. Well, I have to say, that makes sense of a few things.

GABBY. Didn't he mention why he was putting you through the netter?

SAMI. I love him. He's a proper little genius. But I'm horrible to him.

GABBY. Well, maybe you should stop being horrible to him?

SAMI. What, like you? I just tease him. I'd never sleep with his missus. She was crying her eyes out, man, for hours. Poor kid.

Beat.

Is that what you think of me, really? After all these years? I mean, I thought it was just snobbery, possibly a little racism, you looking down on me, like I'm something you should have passed by, someone you should be bossing around /

GABBY. Racism?! / You're calling me racist for thinking you're a fucking dick?!

SAMI. The world's changed. It ain't degrees and all that shit which matters now, it's getting on with the job in hand. Making some money. I mean, one hundred and twenty pounds for a Christmas tree! What idiot pays that for something that sits in their house and dies?

GABBY. Interesting time to get defiant.

SAMI. Fifty pounds.

GABBY. I don't want your money.

SAMI. See that! You're above my money. You think because I want to make some money and be successful I'm just a morally bankrupt arsehole who'd sleep with his cousin's girlfriend and take advantage of a child behind a hut in a car park.

GABBY. You made him clean up sick with his hands.

Beat.

SAMI. You think I went to my imam and said, 'When I grow up I want to sell Christmas trees'? I had dreams, man.

GABBY. Oh, poor Sam! You dreams didn't come true either? Come on then, what were they?

SAMI. I wanted to be a singer innit.

Beat.

GABBY. Can you sing?

SAMI. Yeah.

GABBY. Go on then.

SAMI. Fuck off.

GABBY. Go on. Sing me something good and I'll cut you out.

Of course SAMI *can sing. But he's been up most of the night and he's tied up in tree net. He doesn't acquit himself well.*

I think this job saved you a lot of heartache and rejection.

SAMI. So cut me out, yeah?

GABBY. I said something good.

SAMI. Gabriella! Dammit, let me out, I've got shit to do today! One hundred pounds, final offer.

GABBY. Final time: I don't want your money.

SAMI. Why not? I earned it honestly. It lets me buy my mum nice things and live in a nice house and pay some of Taj's tuition fees – yeah, I do that. Don't tell him. Ever. It's not making the world a worse place, is it? Selling Christmas trees? It makes people happy. People leave here with a smile on their face, don't they?

GABBY. Yes. If I didn't serve them.

Beat.

SAMI. You gonna cut me out then?

GABBY. I told you, knives are like spoons.

GABBY sits down with him.

SAMI. In that case, Gabby, babe, sorry, Gabby, I got to fire you. This time for real. I mean, if you hadn't have given that dude Nick's number then maybe we could have kept it between ourselves, but Nick's involved now. That's not putting kids through the netter, man, that's really psycho shit, shouting and throwing trees around.

GABBY. Yep, I was out of hand.

SAMI. I'm a bit impressed you can break a tree.

GABBY. I was very angry.

SAMI. I don't think of much of this complaining guy whoever he is, talking about pressing assault charges for being threatened physically by a girl.

GABBY. Assault charges?

SAMI. His story's all over the place, kept calling you a 'him'. Joe a 'she'. Something about climbing mountains up the wrong face, I got lost.

Still, I gotta fire you.

GABBY. Sure.

SAMI. Can I fire you from Christmas Day, though, cos I'm not going to find anyone to do today and tomorrow now, am I?

GABBY. You'll give Joe some work next year if he needs it, won't you?

SAMI. I got no complaints about Joe.

GABBY. Thanks. We're not…

SAMI. Course not. He's not blind, is he.

Beat.

This is you putting things right, is it? Get visited by Old Marley last night or something?

A quizzical look from GABBY.

What, I'm not allowed to read now either?

GABBY. Taj withdrew his PhD application because he thought he was in love with Betty.

SAMI. He did what?

GABBY. I tried everything to stop him.

SAMI. It's like the whole last six hours are suddenly *clear*.

Beat.

What we gonna do?

GABBY. 'We'? This is *your* thing to put right.

SAMI. We're his mates, aren't we? What we gonna do?

GABBY. You need to speak to his supervisor, whoever he sent that email to. Can you make it up north today?

SAMI. No, what, to Leeds? No!

GABBY. That's what needs to happen.

SAMI. Today, right, today, after you get me out of seven layers of netting, I have to drive round every outlet in London, a round journey of thirty miles that takes me over ten hours – I don't even know where Leeds is!

GABBY. You get on the M1 and follow the sign that says *North*.

SAMI. I've never been north of Chalk Farm. You see the map after the election? It's all blue from there to Scotland, fucking bandit country.

GABBY. We have to find out who his supervisor is first and then find his home address. You have to turn up on his doorstep.

SAMI. Right, so we need someone with nothing to do, who knows where Leeds is, knows their way round the university, someone who isn't afraid of Tories and could sell sand to the Arabs.

They both arrive at the same solution. They smile.

Give me the phone.

GABBY. I'd like to do it. Please. There's something else I need to say.

'Song Nine' – Sami

Scene Five

Wednesday December 23rd.

JOE *and* GABBY.

JOE. Dad's at Reading.

GABBY. Go on then.

JOE. I can't believe you have to do tomorrow on your own.

GABBY. I love doing Christmas Eve.

JOE. Wonder how she's getting on?

GABBY. She'll nail it.

JOE. I still can't believe you didn't get a photo.

GABBY. People are just a mass of contradictions, aren't they?

Hi there! Still plenty of those and I'm throwing in free reindeer.

Sami's okay. There is a job for you next year. I know it's a long way. But if you wanted to come back to London, you could.

JOE. I haven't even finished packing yet.

GABBY. It's a long drive.

JOE. If you're ever passing through.

GABBY. On my way to Ireland via the sea.

JOE. That's North Wales. Don't go there.

GABBY. Let me know if you can get biscuits at trade – **Yes, we're open until noon tomorrow.**

JOE. **Not me. Driving home for Christmas. Bye now.**

GABBY. **Thank you, bye. Merry Christmas.**

JOE. What was that?

GABBY. What?

JOE. 'Merry Christmas'.

GABBY. I started on that ages ago. It's Christmas-Eve Eve, won't wear it out now.

JOE. How much longer you got?

GABBY. Couple of hours. We could go for a drink if you want to hang on for –

JOE. If he's at Reading he'll only be / another hour.

GABBY. Sure.

JOE. He gets anxious driving back too late.

GABBY. No worries.

JOE. See you next year?

GABBY. **Just take that through to Taj on the till, thank you.**

Oh, yeah, no, you won't see me, I got fired.

JOE. What for?

GABBY. It's a long list.

Yeah, all the wreaths are half-price now.

JOE. What will you do instead?

GABBY. I'll have to get through January to November first.

JOE. You'll be all right.

GABBY. So you keep saying – **Yes, you can have that display one, I'll see if Taj is around to get it for you – maybe pay and I'll get it out for you whilst you're inside. No worries.**

Do you – **That's all we have left** – I was going to say if you're ever – **I'll be there in just a second** – Seeing the guys at Harlequins or whatever. **I'll be right there.**

JOE. I'll call you.

GABBY. Okay – **Yes, they are all non-drop** – What, if you're in London?

JOE. Or just… anyway. If that's /

GABBY. Yeah fine.

I'll be right there.

I should…

JOE. Yeah, sorry.

GABBY. Will you?

JOE. What?

GABBY. Call me? Don't say it if you're not going to, I don't mind. I just can't do any more waiting for the phone to ring.

He kisses her. It's not long. It's not Hollywood. It might not even be on the lips. It's an answer to her question.

TAJ *enters.*

TAJ. I'm cold, there's nothing to do, can I go home?

GABBY. What?

TAJ. Can I go home? They need help.

GABBY. Yeah – **Sorry to keep you waiting.** I have to go and /

JOE. Merry Christmas.

GABBY *smiles. She goes.*

Is that her phone?

TAJ. She just leaves it lying around like she wants it stolen.

JOE. Great.

JOE *picks up her phone and plays with it for a second.*

TAJ. You checking her browsing history?

JOE. –

TAJ. Or what?

JOE. I'm setting a ringtone. Don't tell her. Cheer up, mate, might never happen.

TAJ. I'm decided I'm with Gabby on the whole 'life is completely awful' thing.

JOE. Taj. It isn't. It's the opposite, I promise you.

TAJ. Can you not even switch it off for like ten minutes and be miserable with the rest of us?

JOE. See you later, Taj. It's been fun.

They shake hands. TAJ *throws his arms round* JOE. *It's awkward.* JOE *reaches into his bag and pulls out a beautifully wrapped present.*

Oh shit. Give this to Gabs, would you?

TAJ. What is it?

JOE. It's a Christmas present.

TAJ. Yeah, I can see that, I meant /

JOE. See you, Taj. Cheer up, trust me.

JOE *exits.* TAJ *tries to get into* GABBY*'s present to see what it is.* GABBY *comes back.*

GABBY. Has he gone?

TAJ. He left you this.

GABBY. For me?

TAJ. It's okay, he's gone, open it.

GABBY. No, it's a Christmas present, I have to wait until the day after tomorrow.

TAJ. I want to know what it is.

GABBY. It's not for you. Go serve that customer.

TAJ. You said I could go home.

GABBY. After them.

TAJ. Fine. Don't open it without me.

TAJ *exits.*

GABBY *opens her present. It is a stack of immaculately made and finished 'log-end' coasters. She smiles and she looks over them.*

'Song Ten' – Joe

GABBY. Told you so.

Scene Six

Christmas Eve.

GABBY *is alone at Festive Pines.*

GABBY. **Merry Christmas! Hi there, still some of those left, sure – have a rummage, there are still some good ones. Morning. Merry Christmas.**

TAJ *enters.*

Taj! Did you forget something?

TAJ. I needed to get out the house.

GABBY. It's busy. I'm doing everything half-price because Sami cannot fire me twice. You pitching in or just standing there. You okay?

TAJ. No.

GABBY. What's up?

TAJ. I'm not going to cure cancer.

GABBY. Taj, you're – Help with this, it'll cheer you up.

TAJ. I can't hear that sentence from you, I will hang myself.

GABBY. Okay. Just mope around for a bit here, though, will you? Don't leave.

TAJ. Someone wrote recently that cancer was a good way to die and perhaps we should stop working so hard to cure it. **I don't work here.**

GABBY. **Everything we have left is out**.

TAJ. Ebola's a horrible way to die. Perhaps I could do that.

GABBY. **I prefer the one on the right, it's slimmer at the bottom and I can take those loose bits off if you like.**

TAJ. Gabs?

GABBY. Taj?

TAJ. Why are you so cheerful?

Over his shoulder, GABBY *sees* BETTY *arrive.*

GABBY. It's not just a thing. That can make your soul vibrate. I got that wrong.

TAJ. What?

GABBY. Never mind, it's a Christmas miracle.

TAJ. I'm sorry I said those things about Ed and your job. I didn't mean them.

GABBY. You're one of my very best friends in the whole world.

Ignore the prices, we can work something out, honestly, it's nearly midday.

Taj, just serve that person behind you, would you?

TAJ. I don't work here.

TAJ *sees* BETTY.

What do you want?

BETTY *offers* TAJ *a letter.*

BETTY. I didn't sleep with Sami. By the way.

TAJ. What's that, a DNA test?

BETTY. It's an early Christmas present.

TAJ *takes it. Put it in his back pocket.*

Beat.

Open it then.

TAJ. It's not Christmas yet.

BETTY. Open it. Now.

TAJ. No. You didn't open your present from Joe and I will not be bossed around continually by you women any more.

GABBY. Open the letter, Taj, or we'll net you.

TAJ opens the letter.

He cannot quite believe what he is reading. His relief is overwhelming.

TAJ. How did you do this?

BETTY. Gabby and Sami called and said there was a way to put this right so I took my dad's Jaguar that I was never allowed to drive but it's not his any more it's the bank's so fuck him and I /

Before she can finish TAJ has thrown his arms round her.

TAJ. Thank you.

GABBY *stands awkwardly, looking on.* TAJ *turns and includes her in the hug. The three of them stand holding each other for a moment.*

GABBY. **Yes, they're all non-drop, we only stock non-drop trees!**

BETTY. It's snowing.

They watch it a moment.

TAJ. A Christmas miracle.

GABBY. No, it's just cold as fuck – **Trust me, just hold off five minutes.**

TAJ. Have you got to go back to Eastbourne now?

BETTY. No. We're doing Christmas in our house. Last one.

TAJ. We do Boxing Day curry. Mum never cooks it otherwise cos she won't do the jars and Gran's recipe takes her three days so it's a treat. Come over if you like.

BETTY. Thank you. I'd love that. Has he gone back to Wales?

GABBY. Yes. Why?

BETTY. Well, there's always next year.

GABBY. Not for me there isn't.

BETTY. You'll always have a job here if you want it.

GABBY. Sami –

BETTY. Sami won't be in charge next year.

GABBY. Fair point. Okay, that's it, you doing this with me? One last time?

TAJ. She'll be in Cardiff next year.

GABBY. Yeah, sports journalism.

BETTY. Seriously?

GABBY. No.

TAJ. Why not?

BETTY. Do it. Go to Wales.

GABBY. I can't go to Wales, what for?

TAJ. What for? / Come on.

GABBY. I can't just rock up in Wales and say, 'Hi, I'm that girl you sold trees with I just drove three hundred miles on the off-chance you were free for that casual drink.'

BETTY. It's romantic!

GABBY. I can't just show up!

BETTY. If he just showed up now –

GABBY. Which he won't because he's home already.

BETTY. That would be like *Love Actually*.

GABBY. Just because I'm cheerful doesn't mean I want to be in a Richard Curtis movie.

TAJ. Wuss.

GABBY. I'm not showing up in Wales. Unless I get invited.

BETTY. Yay, she's going to Wales!

GABBY. He hasn't even called, he probably won't and I've hidden my phone in a hay bale so let's stop talking about it – I've always wanted to do this.

TAJ. Do what?

GABBY. You with me?

BETTY. What are we doing?

GABBY. **Everyone, the trees are free, just help yourselves! Take whatever you like, please just help yourselves, make a donation to charity – No really, give it to Crisis or someone – Thank you – Merry Christmas!**

TAJ. **Merry Christmas!**

GABBY. **Happy Christmas!**

TAJ. **Have a great time!**

BETTY. **Merry Christmas!**

GABBY. **Merry Christmas! Take it, my pleasure, really, merry Christmas.**

TAJ. *Feliz Navidad!*

BETTY. *Joyeux Noël!*

GABBY. *Frohe Weihnachten.*

BETTY. **And a Happy New Year!**

GABBY. **Happy Christmas! Merry Christmas, everyone.**

They are having a truly great time.

GABBY*'s phone rings.* The Muppet Show *theme tune.*

She smiles.

End.

www.nickhernbooks.co.uk

facebook.com/nickhernbooks

twitter.com/nickhernbooks